TEACHER'S PET PUBLICATIONS

LITPLAN TEACHER PACK
for
The Pigman's Legacy
based on the book by
Paul Zindel

Written by
Marion B. Hoffman

© 1999 Teacher's Pet Publications
All Rights Reserved

This **LitPlan** on Paul Zindel's **The Pigman's Legacy**
has been brought to you by Teacher's Pet Publications, Inc.

Copyright Teacher's Pet Publications 1999
11504 Hammock Point
Berlin MD 21811

Only the student materials in this unit plan may be
reproduced. Pages such as worksheets and study
guides may be reproduced for use in the purchaser's
classroom. For any additional copyright questions,
contact Teacher's Pet Publications.

Table of Contents - The Pigman's Legacy

Introduction	6
Unit Objectives	9
Reading Assignment Sheet	10
Unit Outline	11
Study Questions (Short Answer)	15
Quiz/Study Questions (Multiple Choice)	26
Pre-reading Vocabulary Worksheets	47
Lesson One (Introductory Lesson)	61
Nonfiction Assignment Sheet	63
Oral Reading Evaluation Form	64
Writing Assignment #1	67
Writing Assignment #2	72
Writing Assignment #3	84
Vocabulary Review Activities	86
Extra Writing Assignments/Discussion ?s	88
Unit Tests	97
Unit Resource Materials	123
Vocabulary Resource Materials	139

A Few Notes About The Author
Paul Zindel

Paul Zindel is an author who understands and enjoys his audience. Not only does he say in interviews that he likes teenagers and feels a special proclivity for them and their lives, but again and again his voice speaks out for teenagers in his books. He has a sense of fun and authenticity about him that young people seem almost universally to respond favorably to.

Zindel was born on Staten Island in New York City in 1936. About the time that he was two years old, his father left the family. Zindel was raised by a single mother.

The fact that they were forced to move a great deal during his childhood may have deprived him of some of the close relationships that children often form. But having so many experiences so young apparently provided him with a storehouse of knowledge gained by observing situations and people along the way. According to Zindel himself, all of his books started with some experience in his own life.

After attending public elementary school in New York, he went on to Port Richmond High School in the same city. It was there that he published his first story collaboratively with a schoolmate. "A Geometric Nightmare" was, not surprisingly, a story that describes a geometry teacher who frightened Zindel and the other student.

Zindel graduated from Wagner College and became a high school chemistry teacher. He taught for ten years before his play, *The Effect of Gamma Rays on Man-in-the-Moon Marigolds* was produced in 1965. At that point he began to dedicate full time to his writing.

Zindel currently lives in Manhattan. He is married and the father of two post-teenage children. He has always had a variety of pets in his life.

Some of Zindel's most noteworthy works, in addition to *Gamma Rays*, for which he won the 1971 Pulitzer Prize and the New York Critics Circle Award, are **The Pigman** (1968), **My Darling, My Hamburger** (1969), **I Never Loved Your Mind** (1970), **Pardon Me, You're Stepping on My Eyeball** (1976), **Confessions of a Teenage Baboon** (1977), **The Undertaker's Gone Bananas** (1978), **The Pigman's Legacy** (1980), **Harry and Hortense at Hormone High** (1984), and **The Amazing and Death-Defying Diary of Eugene Dingman** (1987).

A Few Notes About the Author continued page 2

The Bantam paperback edition of **The Pigman's Legacy** used for this unit plan quotes *Publishers Weekly* on the book's success: "The Zindel style that makes you laugh through tears results in frenzied adventures, enthralling examples of four people armed by love, forcing hard luck to say 'uncle.'"

Perhaps of more genuine interest to young readers, the same paperback says that "Paul Zindel enjoys television, movies, dream interpretation, swimming, and fattening foods—particularly Hunan cuisine and ice cream. He also likes new experiences and teenagers who need someone to confide in."

A great wealth of information is available about Zindel on the internet. Interested readers can even hear a recording of the author's voice. This is a most accessible writer.

Introduction
The Pigman's Legacy

This unit has been designed to develop students' reading, writing, thinking, and language skills through exercises and activities related to **The Pigman's Legacy** by Paul Zindel. It includes eighteen lessons, supported by extra resource materials.

The **introductory lesson** introduces students to one of the themes of the novel (sharing with others and leaving a legacy) through a bulletin board activity. Subsequent lessons focus on such themes as concerns of America's aging population, parent-child relationships, pet ownership, the responsibility of pet ownership, adolescence, and love.

The **reading assignments** are approximately 12 pages each; some are a little shorter while others are a little longer. Students have approximately 15 minutes of pre-reading work to do prior to each reading assignment. This pre-reading work involves reviewing the study questions for the assignment and doing some vocabulary work for 7 to 10 vocabulary words they will encounter in their reading. You may want to ask them to do the vocabulary exercises along with their reading so that they can try to understand the words in context.

The **study guide questions** are fact-based questions; students can find the answers to these questions right in the text. These questions come in two formats: short answer or multiple choice. The best use of these materials is probably to use the short answer version of the questions as study guides for students since answers will be more complete and to use the multiple choice version for occasional quizzes.

The **vocabulary work** is intended to enrich students' vocabularies as well as to aid in the students' understanding of the book. Prior to or along with each reading assignment, students will complete a two-part worksheet for approximately 7 to 10 vocabulary words in the upcoming reading assignment. Part I focuses on students' use of general knowledge and contextual clues by giving the sentence in which the word appears in the text. Students are then to write down what they think the words mean based on the words' usage. Part II nails down the definitions of the words by giving students dictionary definitions of the words and having students match the words to the correct definitions based on the words' contextual usage. Students should then have a thorough understanding of all of the words as they are used in the text.

After each reading assignment, students will go back and formulate answers for the study guide questions. Discussion of these questions serves as a **review** of the most important events and ideas presented in the reading assignments.

After students complete extra discussion questions, there is a **vocabulary review** lesson which pulls together all of the fragmented vocabulary lists for the reading assignments and gives students a review of all of the words they have studied.

Pigman's Legacy Introduction page 2

Following the reading of the book, two lessons are devoted to the **extra discussion questions/writing assignments**. These questions focus on interpretation, critical analysis, and personal response, employing a variety of thinking skills and adding to the students' understanding of the novel. These questions may be done as a **group activity**. Using the information they have acquired so far through individual work and class discussions, students may get together to further examine the text and to brainstorm ideas relating to the themes of the novel.

The group activity is followed by a **reports and discussion** session in which the groups share their ideas about the book with the entire class; thus, the entire class gets exposed to many different ideas regarding the themes and events of the book.

There are three **writing assignments** in this unit, each with the purpose of informing, persuading, or expressing personal opinions. The first assignment is to write from personal experience: is true love possible at age sixteen? This assignment helps students to relate at least one of the ideas in **The Pigman's Legacy** to their own lives. It also helps them to express logical views on a topic that generally is approached only emotionally. The second assignment gives students the opportunity to inform. Derived from the Colonel's Game of Life in **The Pigman's Legacy**, students are to devise their own game of life and to inform readers of how to play it. This assignment will underscore what students have already read and cause them to move from the text to their own ideas about life. The third assignment is to give students a chance to persuade: students are given six choices of possible arguments. All are based on the book.

In addition, there is a **nonfiction reading assignment**. Students are required to read a piece of nonfiction related in some way to **The Pigman's Legacy**. After reading their nonfiction pieces, students will fill out a worksheet on which they answer questions regarding facts, interpretation, criticism, and personal opinions. During one class period, students make **oral presentations** about the nonfiction pieces they have read. This not only exposes all students to a wealth of information, but it also gives students the opportunity to practice public speaking.

There is an optional **class project** (Project Aging) through which students gain first-hand knowledge of the situation of America's aging population and are offered ways to take part in helping to do something about the concerns of this group of citizens.

The **review lesson** pulls together all aspects of the unit. The teacher is given four or five choices of activities or games to use which all serve the same basic function of reviewing all of the information presented in the unit.

Pigman's Legacy Introduction page 3

The **unit test** comes in three separate formats:
matching/short answer/essay/vocabulary (2 tests)
matching/multiple choice/essay/vocabulary (2 tests)
matching/short answer critical thinking/essay/vocabulary (1 advanced test)

Also in this unit is a **resource section** with suggestions for an in-class library, crossword and word search puzzles related to **The Pigman's Legacy**, and extra vocabulary worksheets. There is a list of **bulletin board ideas** which gives suggestions for bulletin boards to go along with this unit. In addition, there is a list of **extra class activities** the teacher could use to enhance the unit or as a substitution for an exercise the teacher feels is inappropriate for his or her class.

Answer keys are located directly after the **reproducible student materials** throughout the unit. The student materials may be reproduced for use in the teacher's classroom without infringement of copyright. No other portion of this unit may be reproduced without the written consent of Teacher's Pet Publications, Inc.

Unit Objectives - The Pigman's Legacy

1. Through reading Paul Zindel's **The Pigman's Legacy**, students will gain better understanding of some of the themes of the book: friendship, concerns of growing older in America, trust, caring for pets, concerns of adolescence, death and dying, and different types of love.

2. Students will demonstrate their understanding of the text on four levels: factual, interpretive, critical, and personal.

3. Students will define their own viewpoints about the aforementioned themes and will be encouraged to examine character motivation and development.

4. Students will be exposed to some of the concerns of America's aging population, spending some time thinking about how older people feel about themselves and are treated by others as well as the societal concerns that impact on their later years.

5. Students may undertake a project designed to help them to better understand aging in America and perhaps to contribute to solving some of the problems facing older people.

6. Students will be given the opportunity to practice reading aloud and silently to improve their skills in each area.

7. Students will answer questions to demonstrate their knowledge and understanding of the main events and characters in **The Pigman's Legacy**.

8. Students will enrich their vocabularies and improve their understanding of the book through the vocabulary lessons prepared for use in conjunction with the book.

9. The writing assignments in this unit have several purposes:
   a.. To have students demonstrate the ability to inform, to persuade, and/or to express their own ideas.
   > Note: Students will demonstrate ability to write effectively <u>to inform</u> by developing and organizing facts to convey information; <u>to persuade</u> by choosing a strong purpose for arguing a point of view, by selecting and organizing information, and by designing appropriate strategies for conveying their main points; and <u>to express personal ideas</u> by evaluating characters, situations, and/or plot from their own points of view.

   b. To check students' reading comprehension
   c. To make students think about the ideas presented in the book they are reading
   d. To encourage logical thinking
   e. To provide an opportunity to practice good grammar and improve students' use of the English language

Reading Assignment Sheet
The Pigman's Legacy

Section of the Text Assigned	Date Assigned	Date to be Completed
The Promise + Chapters One and Two		
Chapters Three and Four		
Chapter Five		
Chapter Six		
Chapters Seven and Eight		
Chapters Nine and Ten		
Chapter Eleven		
Chapter Twelve		
Chapters Thirteen and Fourteen		

Unit Outline
The Pigman's Legacy

1 Introduction Distribution PV "Promise" & Ch 3 & 4	2 Read "Promise" & Ch 1 & 2 PV 3 & 4	3 Review Ch 1 & 2 Read Ch 3 & 4 PVR Ch 5 WA#1 (opinion)	4 Review Ch 3, 4, 5 PV Ch 6 Assign R Ch 6 Group activity	5 Review Ch 6 PV Ch 7 & 8 WA#2 (inform)
6 Review 7 & 8 PVR Ch 9 & 10 Prep for reading assign.	7 Nonfiction Reading Assign.	8 Review Ch 9 & 10 PVR 11 Set up Project Aging	9 PVR 12 Review through Ch 12	10 Role playing exercise
11 PVR Ch 13 & 14	12 Review through Ch 14 Project updates or MC quizzes WA#3 (persuade)	13 Vocabulary review	14 Extra Discussion Questions/Wrtg Assign. Discussion Critical thinking Relate book to own lives	15 Review ideas through use of Quotations Worksheets
16 Project updates or Brainstorming exercise	17 Report on NF Reading Assign. Broaden knowledge of topics Prep for Unit Tests	18 UNIT TESTS		

STUDY GUIDE QUESTIONS

Short Answer Study Questions - The Pigman's Legacy

The Promise and Chapters One and Two

1. What information about John and Lorraine is explained in the book's preface, called The Promise?
2. In the first chapter of the book, told from John's point of view, what does he tell the reader about his practical jokes?
3. What does John think about writing book reports for his English class?
4. How does John demonstrate mild and horrendous curses?
5. How much does John think the readers of **The Pigman's Legacy** have to know about the original book, **The Pigman**?
6. Who tells the story in Chapter Two?
7. What gift do mean people say John and Lorraine gave the original Pigman?
8. What does the Pigman kill, according to Lorraine?
9. What are the two legacies that Lorraine thinks can be left by a Pigman?
10. What was located right across the street from the original Pigman's house?
11. What do John and Lorraine discover at the home of the original Pigman?
12. What was the original Pigman's real name?

Chapters Three and Four
1. Why does John think that psychologists go into psychology in the first place?
2. What was unusual about the way that Dolly Racinski dressed?
3. What kind of help did John and Lorraine expect to get from the adult world?
4. What terms does John use for his mother and father?
5. What job does Dolly Racinski do at the high school?
6. What kind of cigarettes does Lorraine want John to smoke?
7. What does John say kids can do to impress their parents?
8. Why does the man living in the Pigman's house drink acidophilus milk?
9. Why does Dolly especially like John and Lorraine?
10. Why does Lorraine think Mr. Pignati has come back from the dead?

Chapter Five
1. When the old man first meets John and Lorraine, who does he think they are?
2. Why did John decide to show the old man some respect?
3. Why do John and Lorraine try to check the old man's pulse?
4. What does John tell his parents when they ask why he is depressed?
5. What present did John and Lorraine take to the old man when they returned?

Pigman's Legacy Short Answer Study Questions page 2

Chapter Six
1. Why did John and Lorraine say that they have returned to see the old man?
2. What was the old man wearing around his neck?
3. A part of what animal was on the old man's medallion?
4. What was engraved on the medallion?
5. Why was Colonel Parker Glenville knighted by the King of Sweden?
6. Why does John say that the old man should look at him and Lorraine?
7. What does the old man say is the only game he knows?
8. What happens when John describes what he sees while playing the Game of Life?
9. What does John's Cup of Love look like?
10. Why has Lorraine's mother taught her daughter so many negative things about boys?
11. What did the old man tell John the tree in the road represented?
12. What is the wall the old man says is blocking John's way on the road?

Chapters Seven and Eight
1. What does the old man say his name is?
2. What is the old man's car like?
3. What has John's driving experience been prior to driving the old man's car?
4. What does John tell Lorraine to do once it starts to rain?
5. How did the old man, John, and Lorraine get into the town house?
6. What were on the three large plaques that were in the town house?
7. How did John and Lorraine discover the old man's true identity?
8. Who was the old man really?
9. Who did the German shepherd who got into the car belong to?
10. What was the German shepherd's name?

Chapters Nine and Ten
1. How did the German shepherd wake up the Colonel?
2. Why did John and Lorraine take the Colonel to the hospital?
3. How did John, Lorraine, and the Colonel get out of the hospital?
4. What kind of physical relationship do John's parents have?
5. How had the Colonel and his dog been separated?
6. Why was the Colonel in trouble with the IRS?
7. What does Dolly always say when asked how she is?
8. What adult do John and Lorraine recruit to help them?
9. What medical condition is the Colonel suffering from?
10. What big announcement does Dolly make when John and Lorraine return?

Pigman's Legacy Short Answer Study Questions page 3

Chapter Eleven
1. Why does Dolly say that the Colonel should be allowed to go to Atlantic City?
2. What did the Colonel sell to raise money to go to Atlantic City?
3. What two reasons does the Colonel give for not taking Gus along to Atlantic City?
4. How much money was the Colonel's collection of silver dollars worth on the Silver Exchange?
5. How did the Colonel spend a lot of quarters **on the way to** Atlantic City?
6. What nice thing did Dolly keep saying about John and Lorraine?
7. When Dolly played the Game of Life with the Colonel, what did she say she would do when she got to the Wall of Death?
8. Why did Dolly say she responded this way to the idea of the Wall of Death?
9. What was going on in the "special restaurant" that the parking valets referred the Colonel to?
10. How much money did Dolly and the Colonel win at the blackjack table?
11. What did Dolly ask John to do with the money she and the Colonel won?
12. What did John ultimately do with the money the Colonel and Dolly won?

Chapter Twelve
1. Who finally told Dolly and the Colonel about their lost money?
2. After she got over her initial shock, how did Dolly respond to losing the money?
3. What was the Colonel's response when John and Lorraine offered to pay back his money by cleaning his house and bringing him food?
4. What present did the Colonel give to Dolly as they returned home from Atlantic City?
5. What does Lorraine learn from watching how supportive Dolly is of the Colonel?
6. What happened to the Colonel in the car returning from Atlantic City?

Chapters Thirteen and Fourteen
1. What did Dolly, John, and Lorraine do to help the Colonel when he got sick again?
2. What revelation does Dolly make about the Colonel's medical condition?
3. What announcement does the Colonel make at the hospital?
4. What request does the Colonel make at the hospital?
5. Why did John decide to take Gus along to the hospital?
6. What did Gus do when he found the Colonel at the hospital?
7. What happened to Gus at the end of the book?
8. What was on the floor of the hospital where Lorraine stopped the elevator?
9. What does John say to Lorraine at the end of the book?
10. What was the legacy of John and Lorraine's Pigman?

Key: Short Answer Study Questions - The Pigman's Legacy

<u>The Promise and Chapters One and Two</u>

1. What information about John and Lorraine is explained in the book's preface, called The Promise?
   The information is that John and Lorraine are now honestly telling their story about the Pigman.

2. In the first chapter of the book, told from John's point of view, what does he tell the reader about his practical jokes?
   John says that although he still jokes around, he has given up most of his practical jokes.

3. What does John think about writing book reports for his English class?
   John hates writing book reports and chooses only the thinnest books possible to report on.

4. How does John demonstrate mild and horrendous curses?
   He uses @#$% for a mild curse and 3@#$% for a horrendous one.

5. How much does John think the readers of **The Pigman's Legacy** have to know about the original book, **The Pigman**?
   He says that the reader of **The Pigman's Legacy** doesn't need to know much about the earlier book.

6. Who tells the story in Chapter Two?
   Lorraine tells the story in Chapter Two.

7. What gift do mean people say John and Lorraine gave the original Pigman?
   They say that John and Lorraine gave the Pigman "death."

8. What does the Pigman kill, according to Lorraine?
   The Pigman kills a person's childhood.

9. What are the two legacies that Lorraine thinks can be left by a Pigman?
   He can leave the legacy of life or the legacy of death.

10. What was located right across the street from the original Pigman's house?
    A convent was located right across the street.

11. What do John and Lorraine discover at the home of the original Pigman?
They discover that a hobo has moved into the house.

12. What was the original Pigman's real name?
His name was Mr. Pignati.

Chapters Three and Four
1. Why does John think that psychologists go into psychology in the first place?
He thinks that they go into psychology because they are screwballs.

2. What was especially unusual about the way that Dolly Racinski dressed?
Dolly wore giant-sized pom-pom-shaped rhinestone earrings.

3. What kind of help did John and Lorraine expect to get from the adult world?
They expected to get no help at all.

4. What terms does John use for his mother and father?
John refers to his mother as the Old Lady and to his father as Bore.

5. What job does Dolly Racinski do at the high school?
Dolly is a cafeteria-floor sweeper.

6. What kind of cigarettes does Lorraine want John to smoke?
She wants him to smoke spinach cigarettes.

7. What does John say kids can do to impress their parents?
John says they can do chores like carrying their dishes out to the kitchen and occasionally washing their own dishes and taking out the trash.

8. Why does the man living in the Pigman's house drink acidophilus milk?
He drinks acidophilus milk because he has intestinal problems.

9. Why does Dolly especially like John and Lorraine?
She especially likes them because they are kind to her.

10. Why does Lorraine think Mr. Pignati has come back from the dead?
She thinks he has come back to give her and John a message.

Pigman's Legacy Key: Short Answer Study Questions page 3

Chapter Five

1. When the old man first meets John and Lorraine, who does he think they are?
   He thinks they are representatives from the IRS.

2. Why did John decide to show the old man some respect?
   He decided to show him some respect because of his age.

3. Why do John and Lorraine try to check the old man's pulse?
   They try to check his pulse because they think he is dead.

4. What does John tell his parents when they ask why he is depressed?
   He says that he is tired.

5. What present did John and Lorraine take to the old man when they returned?
   They took him some marble pecan fudge.

Chapter Six

1. Why did John and Lorraine say that they have returned to see the old man?
   They say that they are being nice and trying to help him.

2. What does the old man wear around his neck?
   He wears a medallion that is a fossil.

3. A part of what animal was on the old man's medallion?
   It is the horn of a rhino.

4. What was engraved on the medallion?
   Engraved on the medallion was *To the Colonel, for fifty years of service*.

5. Why was Colonel Parker Glenville knighted by the King of Sweden?
   Colonel Parker Glenville was knighted for the subway system he designed in Stockholm.

6. Why does John say that the old man should look at him and Lorraine?
   He says that he and Lorraine want to be the old man's friends.

7. What does the old man say is the only game he knows?
   He says the only game he knows is The Game of Life.

Pigman's Legacy Key Short Answer Study Questions page 4

8. What happens when John describes what he sees while playing The Game of Life?
   The old man interprets the meaning of what John sees.

9. What does John's Cup of Love look like?
   The Cup is Styrofoam, like the kind a person gets at a hot-dog stand.

10. Why has Lorraine's mother taught her daughter so many negative things about boys?
    Her mother was bitter because her husband left her shortly after Lorraine was born.

11. What did the old man tell John the tree in the road represented?
    He said that the tree was John's sex life.

12. What is the wall the old man says is blocking John's way on the road?
    The old man says the wall of death is blocking John's way.

Chapters Seven and Eight

1. What does the old man say his name is?
   He says his name is Gus.

2. What is the old man's car like?
   His car is a terrific beat-up canary-yellow old Studebaker convertible.

3. What has John's driving experience been prior to driving the old man's car?
   His only experience has been backing his father's car out of the driveway.

4. What does John tell Lorraine to do once it starts to rain?
   He tells her to put up an umbrella.

5. How did the old man, John, and Lorraine get into the town house?
   The old man threw a trash can through a window.

6. What were on the three large plaques that were in the town house?
   There were dinosaurs on the plaques.

7. How did John and Lorraine discover the old man's true identity?
   They found a picture of him.

8. Who was the old man really?
   The old man was really Colonel Parker Glenville.

Pigman's Legacy Key: Short Answer Study Questions page 5

9. Who did the German shepherd who got into the car belong to?
   The German shepherd belonged to Colonel Glenville.

10. What was the German shepherd's name?
    The German shepherd's name was Gus.

Chapters Nine and Ten

1. How did the German shepherd wake up the Colonel?
   He woke the Colonel up by licking his face.

2. Why did John and Lorraine take the Colonel to the hospital?
   They took him to the hospital because he said he was in terrible pain.

3. How did John, Lorraine, and the Colonel get out of the hospital?
   They all slipped out the door and drove away in the Studebaker.

4. What kind of physical relationship do John's parents have?
   John's parents do not touch each other at all.

5. How had the Colonel and his dog been separated?
   When the Colonel had been forced to leave his home suddenly, he was unable to find Gus.

6. Why was the Colonel in trouble with the IRS?
   He had not paid his taxes for many years.

7. What does Dolly always say when asked how she is?
   Dolly always says, "Lookin' up."

8. What adult do John and Lorraine recruit to help them?
   They recruit Dolly to help them.

9. What medical condition is the Colonel suffering from?
   He has diverticulosis.

10. What big announcement does Dolly make when John and Lorraine return?
    She announces that they are all going to Atlantic City.

Chapter Eleven

1. Why does Dolly say that the Colonel should be allowed to go to Atlantic City?
   She said that it was what he wanted.

2. What did the Colonel sell to raise money to go to Atlantic City?
   He sold his collection of silver dollars.

3. What two reasons does the Colonel give for not taking Gus along to Atlantic City?
   He would have to be left locked up in the car and he (the Colonel) had already lost him once and didn't want to risk losing him again.

4. How much money was the Colonel's collection of silver dollars worth on the Silver Exchange?
   His one hundred twenty-three silver dollars were worth over six hundred dollars.

5. How did the Colonel spend a lot of quarters **on the way to** Atlantic City?
   He spent them at toll booths along the way.

6. What nice thing did Dolly keep saying about John and Lorraine?
   She kept saying, "You kids are just *swell*!"

7. When Dolly played the Game of Life with the Colonel, what did she say she would do when she got to the Wall of Death?
   She said she would fall on her knees and kiss it.

8. Why did Dolly say she responded this way to the idea of the Wall of Death?
   She said she responded this way because she was religious and so wasn't afraid of dying.

9. What was going on in the "special restaurant" that the parking valets referred the Colonel to?
   The customers in the "special restaurant" were gambling.

10. How much money did Dolly and the Colonel win at the blackjack table?
    They won four thousand dollars.

11. What did Dolly ask John to do with the money she and the Colonel won?
    Dolly asked John to put it in his jeans pocket for safekeeping.

12. What did John ultimately do with the money?
    John lost the money gambling.

Chapter Twelve
1. Who finally told Dolly and the Colonel about their lost money?
   Lorraine finally told them.

2. After she got over her initial shock, how did Dolly respond to losing the money?
   Dolly said that it was all right and John shouldn't worry about it.

3. What was the Colonel's response when John and Lorraine offered to pay back his money by cleaning his house and bringing him food?
   He said they didn't have to do that.

4. What present did the Colonel give to Dolly as they returned home from Atlantic City?
   He gave her his special medallion.

5. What does Lorraine learn from watching how supportive Dolly is of the Colonel?
   She learns that she should be more supportive of John when he is troubled.

6. What happened to the Colonel in the car returning from Atlantic City?
   The Colonel became very sick again.

Chapters Thirteen and Fourteen
1. What did Dolly, John, and Lorraine do to help the Colonel when he got sick again?
   They took him to a hospital.

2. What revelation does Dolly make about the Colonel's medical condition?
   She reveals that he is dying.

3. What announcement does the Colonel make at the hospital?
   He announces that he wants to marry Dolly.

4. What request does the Colonel make at the hospital?
   He asks for a priest to marry him and Dolly.

Pigman's Legacy Key: Short Answer Study Questions page 8

5. Why did John decide to take Gus along to the hospital?
   He decided to take Gus along because the dog was trying to throw himself through a window to get out and John was afraid he would be cut on the glass.

6. What did Gus do when he found the Colonel at the hospital?
   He jumped up on the bed and licked the dead Colonel's face.

7. What happened to Gus at the end of the book?
   Dolly decided that she would keep Gus with her.

8. What was on the floor of the hospital where Lorraine stopped the elevator?
   There were many newborn babies on the floor where Lorraine stopped the elevator.

9. What does John say to Lorraine at the end of the book?
   He says, "I want to spend my life with you."

10. What was the legacy of John and Lorraine's Pigman?
    The legacy of the Pigman was love.

Multiple Choice Quizzes - The Pigman's Legacy

<u>The Promise and Chapters One and Two</u>

1. What information about John and Lorraine is explained in the book's preface, called The Promise?
    a. That they are secretly planning to get married soon
    b. That they are now honestly telling their story about the Pigman
    c. That they took part in a plot to kill the old Pigman
    d. That they are planning to run away from home together

2. In the first chapter of the book, told from John's point of view, what does he tell the reader about his practical jokes?
    a. He says that he has only given up on one practical joke.
    b. He says that he once played an enormous practical joke on Lorraine.
    c. He says that Lorraine has threatened to hit him if he plays any more practical jokes.
    d. He says that although he still jokes around, he has given up most of his practical jokes.

3. What does John think about writing book reports for his English class?
    a. It is one of his favorite assignments in school.
    b. He hates writing book reports and chooses only the thinnest books possible to report on.
    c. He likes to do book reports only on long, complicated books.
    d. He thinks the teachers assign them as busy work for the students.

4. How does John demonstrate mild and horrendous curses?
    a. He says "holy smoke" for a mild curse and "golly gee" for a horrendous one.
    b. He uses @#$% for a mild curse and 3@#$% for a horrendous one.
    c. He crosses his fingers when he says a mild curse and throws his hands into the air when he says a horrendous one.
    d. He says "damn" for a mild curse and "double damn" for a horrendous one.

Pigman's Legacy Multiple Choice Quizzes page 2

5. How much does John think the readers of **The Pigman's Legacy** have to know about the original book, **The Pigman**?
   a. If they didn't read the first book, they won't understand the sequel.
   b. The reader of **The Pigman's Legacy** doesn't need to know much about the earlier book.
   c. If they at least saw the movie based on **The Pigman**, then they will understand the sequel.
   d. They will have a hard time understanding the sequel unless they read the special update on the back cover of **The Pigman's Legacy**.

6. Who tells the story in Chapter Two?
   a. John's teacher
   b. John
   c. Lorraine
   d. The Pigman

7. What gift do mean people say John and Lorraine gave the original Pigman?
   a. "Death"
   b. Lots of happiness
   c. A new car
   d. The keys to an apartment

8. What does the Pigman kill, according to Lorraine?
   a. John and Lorraine's pet rabbit
   b. A person's childhood
   c. His next door neighbor
   d. His wife

9. What are the two legacies that Lorraine thinks can be left by a Pigman?
   a. Lots of money and lots of grief
   b. Love or hatred
   c. Good health or bad health
   d. The legacy of life or the legacy of death

10. What was located right across the street from the original Pigman's house?
    a. a huge pig farm
    b. a convent
    c. a cemetery
    d. John and Lorraine's house

Pigman's Legacy Multiple Choice Quizzes page 3

11. What do John and Lorraine discover at the home of the original Pigman?
    a. That a hobo has moved into the house
    b. That the original Pigman left behind a lot of money
    c. That the original Pigman left them a special note
    d. That several pigeons are living in the house

12. What was the original Pigman's real name?
    a. Joe
    b. Mr. Pigman
    c. Peter Pigman
    d. Mr. Pignati

Pigman's Legacy Multiple Choice Quizzes page 4

Chapters Three and Four
1. Why does John think that psychologists go into psychology in the first place?
   a. Because they are greedy
   b. Because they are screwballs
   c. Because they have good hearts
   d. Because they have a special understanding of human motivation

2. What was unusual about the way that Dolly Racinski dressed?
   a. She always wore worn-out slacks and a white shirt.
   b. She wore giant-sized pom-pom-shaped rhinestone earrings.
   c. She wore a huge gold cross.
   d. She wore a very large blue ring.

3. What kind of help did John and Lorraine expect to get from the adult world?
   a. Only expert, caring help
   b. No help at all
   c. Some help if they asked for it carefully
   d. Some help if they hadn't done anything illegal

4. What terms does John use for his mother and father?
   a. Ma and Pa
   b. The Old Lady and Bore
   c. Carol and Jim
   d. Mama and Papa

5. What job does Dolly Racinski do at the high school?
   a. She is the principal.
   b. She is a substitute teacher.
   c. She is a cafeteria-floor sweeper.
   d. She drives a bus.

6. What kind of cigarettes does Lorraine want John to smoke?
   a. L & M's
   b. spinach
   c. marijuana
   d. Camels

Pigman's Legacy Multiple Choice Quizzes page 5

7. Why does the man living in the Pigman's house drink acidophilus milk?
   a. Because the old Pigman left some in the refrigerator
   b. Because he is a diabetic
   c. Because he is allergic to the other kinds
   d. Because he has intestinal problems

8. What does John say kids can do to impress their parents?
   a. Stay out of trouble
   b. Do chores like carrying their dishes out to the kitchen and occasionally washing their own dishes and taking out the trash
   c. Never get in trouble with the law
   d. Go to bed when they are told and get up in the morning when they are first called

9. Why does Dolly especially like John and Lorraine?
   a. Because they are kind to her
   b. Because they like her special earrings
   c. Because they call her Mrs. Racinski
   d. Because they bring her gifts every Friday

10. Why does Lorraine think Mr. Pignati has come back from the dead?
    a. To give her and John a message
    b. To get revenge on his enemies
    c. To teach them a lesson about practical jokes
    d. To find out why he died in the first place

Pigman's Legacy Multiple Choice Quizzes page 6

Chapter Five
1. When the old man first meets John and Lorraine, who does he think they are?
    a. A couple of trouble makers from the city
    b. Representatives from the IRS
    c. Bill collectors
    d. Members of the local church

2. Why did John decide to show the old man some respect?
    a. Because he got tired of arguing with him
    b. Because of his age
    c. Because the old man seemed really smart
    d. Because the old man threatened him

3. Why do John and Lorraine try to check the old man's pulse?
    a. Because the old man complains that his pulse was racing
    b. Because they think he is dead
    c. Because Lorraine wants to be a doctor
    d. Because they are trying to scare him into having a heart attack

4. What does John tell his parents when they ask why he is depressed?
    a. Because his rabbit died
    b. Because he lost his best friend
    c. Because Lorraine won't go out with him
    d. Because he is tired

5. What present did John and Lorraine take to the old man when they returned?
    a. A bagel
    b. A bag of groceries
    c. Some marble pecan fudge
    d. A pack of cigarettes

Pigman's Legacy Multiple Choice Quizzes page 6

Chapter Six
1. Why did John and Lorraine say that they have returned to see the old man?
    a. They say that they are being nice and trying to help him.
    b. They say that they are curious about what he has done to the house.
    c. They say that they are thinking of calling the police about him.
    d. They say that they want some money from him.

2. What was the old man wearing around his neck?
    a. A gold chain
    b. A picture of his lost love
    c. A special ring
    d. A medallion that is a fossil

3. A part of what animal was on the old man's medallion?
    a. A horse
    b. A dog
    c. A cat
    d. A rhino

4. What was engraved on the medallion?
    a. *To Jim with all my love, Mary*
    b. *To the Colonel, for fifty years of service*
    c. *Many years of service make a great hero*
    d. *Think about me always*

5. Why was Colonel Parker Glenville knighted by the King of Sweden?
    a. For his valor in battle
    b. For the subway system he designed in Stockholm
    c. For personal services beyond the call of duty
    d. For 50 years of teaching

6. Why does John say that the old man should look at him and Lorraine?
    a. Because he always looks down at the floor and it is disconcerting
    b. Because he and Lorraine want to be the old man's friends
    c. Because it is impolite not to look at people who are talking to you
    d. Because they want him to recognize them when they return

7. What does the old man say is the only game he knows?
   a. Chess
   b. Mahjong
   c. The Game of Life
   d. Football

8. What happens when John describes what he sees while playing The Game of Life?
   a. The old man laughs at every one of his responses.
   b. The old man scores his answers each time.
   c. The old man interprets the meaning of what John sees.
   d. Lorraine has to guess what John is describing.

9. What does John's Cup of Love look like?
   a. It is very beautiful and made of bone china.
   b. It is filled with various Disney characters.
   c. It is Styrofoam, like the kind a person gets at a hot-dog stand.
   d. It is gold and very, very heavy.

10. Why has Lorraine's mother taught her daughter so many negative things about boys?
    a. Because she hopes to scare Lorraine into staying away from boys
    b. Because her own brother got into a lot of trouble when he was a boy
    c. Because she thinks John is an especially bad influence on Lorraine
    d. Because she is bitter because her husband left her shortly after Lorraine was born

11. What did the old man tell John the tree in the road represented?
    a. A barrier to John's future success
    b. John's sex life
    c. John's life line
    d. John's future life with Lorraine

12. What is the wall the old man says is blocking John's way on the road?
    a. The old man says the wall of death is blocking John's way.
    b. The old man says that John's lack of sexual experience is blocking his way.
    c. The old man says that John's inhibitions are blocking his way.
    d. The old man says that thoughts of girls are blocking John's way.

Pigman's Legacy Multiple Choice Quizzes page 9

Chapters Seven and Eight

1. What does the old man say his name is?
    a. Michael
    b. Angelo
    c. Gus
    d. Zeke

2. What is the old man's car like?
    a. It is a shiny new BMW convertible.
    b. It is an old Volkswagen bus.
    c. It is a late-model van.
    d. It is a terrific beat-up canary-yellow old Studebaker convertible.

3. What has John's driving experience been prior to driving the old man's car?
    a. He once drove into New York City.
    b. He has backed his father's car out of the driveway.
    c. He has driven but only with a veteran driver in the car with him.
    d. He has driven only about 100 miles around town.

4. What does John tell Lorraine to do once it starts to rain?
    a. Put the top back up
    b. Put up an umbrella
    c. Get out and walk
    d. Put on a hat

5. How did the old man, John, and Lorraine get into the town house?
    a. They walked right in the front door.
    b. They picked a back door lock.
    c. They climbed in a first-floor window.
    d. The old man threw a trash can through a window.

6. What were on the three large plaques that were in the town house?
    a. Pictures of old war heroes
    b. Dinosaurs
    c. Pictures of British royalty
    d. Congratulatory notes to the Colonel

Pigman's Legacy Multiple Choice Quizzes page 10

7. How did John and Lorraine discover the old man's true identity?
   a. He finally told them who he was.
   b. They found a picture of him.
   c. He made a mistake and let them see his driver's license.
   d. He translated a special message that gave away his true identity.

8. Who was the old man really?
   a. An escaped convict
   b. Colonel Parker Glenville
   c. A manservant to Colonel Parker Glenville
   d. A mental patient

9. Who did the German shepherd who got into the car belong to?
   a. Colonel Glenville
   b. The old man's sister
   c. The man who owned the car before the Colonel bought it
   d. The man who lived across the street from where the car was parked

10. What was the German shepherd's name?
    a. Rover
    b. Duke
    c. Lady
    d. Gus

Chapters Nine and Ten

1. How did the German shepherd wake up the Colonel?
    a. He barked really loudly.
    b. He howled.
    c. He licked the Colonel's face.
    d. He whined for a long time.

2. Why did John and Lorraine take the Colonel to the hospital?
    a. Because they thought he was having a heart attack
    b. Because he was in terrible pain
    c. Because he asked them to
    d. Because he had eaten some bad food

3. How did John, Lorraine, and the Colonel get out of the hospital?
    a. The Colonel was discharged and John and Lorraine took him home.
    b. They all slipped out the door and drove away in the Studebaker.
    c. They posed as doctors.
    d. They posed as nurses.

4. What kind of physical relationship do John's parents have?
    a. They touch and hug constantly.
    b. They do not touch each other at all.
    c. They kiss often in public.
    d. They hold hands when they go to the store.

5. How had the Colonel and his dog been separated?
    a. The Colonel was mean to the dog and the dog ran away.
    b. The dog catcher had picked the dog up.
    c. A professional dognapper had stolen the dog.
    d. When the Colonel had been forced to leave his home suddenly, he was unable to find the dog.

6. Why was the Colonel in trouble with the IRS?
    a. Because he forgot to pay his taxes the year before
    b. Because he had not paid his taxes for many years
    c. Because he lied about his income
    d. Because he lied about charitable deductions

Pigman's Legacy Multiple Choice Quizzes page 12

7. What does Dolly always say when asked how she is?
    a. "Golly, I'm just fine."
    b. "Lookin' up."
    c. "Feeling great today."
    d. "Not so good but gettin' better."

8. What adult do John and Lorraine recruit to help them?
    a. John's mother
    b. John's father
    c. Dolly Racinski
    d. Mr. Pignati

9. What medical condition is the Colonel suffering from?
    a. Heart problems
    b. Measles
    c. Diverticulosis
    d. Old age

10. What big announcement does Dolly make when John and Lorraine return?
    a. That they are all going to Atlantic City
    b. That she and the Colonel are going to be married
    c. That she is really a member of the royal family of England
    d. That she is really from Boston

Pigman's Legacy Multiple Choice Quizzes page 13

Chapter Eleven

1. Why does Dolly say that the Colonel should be allowed to go to Atlantic City?
    a. Because he is old and has never before gambled
    b. Because he is a very good gambler
    c. Because he is a winning blackjack player
    d. Because it is what he wanted

2. What did the Colonel sell to raise money to go to Atlantic City?
    a. His special necklace
    b. Some magic beans
    c. A special token given to him by the King of Sweden
    d. His collection of silver dollars

3. What two reasons does the Colonel give for not taking Gus along to Atlantic City?
    a. Gus eats too much.
    b. Gus would get out of the car and want to gamble.
    c. Gus is too mouthy.
    d. Gus would have to be left locked up in the car and he (the Colonel) had already lost him once and didn't want to risk losing him again.

4. How much money was the Colonel's collection of silver dollars worth on the Silver Exchange?
    a. $52.99
    b. Over $600.00
    c. 10 thousand dollars
    d. $127.89

5. How did the Colonel spend a lot of quarters **on the way to** Atlantic City?
    a. He gave them to needy people along the way.
    b. He kept betting store owners that he knew certain things.
    c. He spent them at toll booths along the way.
    d. He kept using them to call home.

6. What nice thing did Dolly keep saying about John and Lorraine?
    a. "You kids are just *swell*!"
    b. "I just *love* you guys."
    c. "You kids are too much!"
    d. "You two remind me of my grandchildren."

Pigman's Legacy Multiple Choice Quizzes page 14

7. When Dolly played the Game of Life with the Colonel, what did she say she would do when she got to the Wall of Death?
   a. Fall on her knees and kiss it
   b. Collapse and cry
   c. Yell for help
   d. Kneel and pray

8. Why did Dolly say she responded this way to the idea of the Wall of Death?
   a. Because she thought everything the Colonel said was too melodramatic
   b. Because she was religious and so wasn't afraid of dying
   c. Because she had tried to think up a particularly dramatic response
   d. Because getting to a Wall of Death wasn't at all like actually meeting Death

9. What was going on in the "special restaurant" that the parking valets referred the Colonel to?
   a. Gambling
   b. Dancing
   c. Eating, drinking, and singing
   d. Illegal drug dealing

10. How much money did Dolly and the Colonel win at the blackjack table?
    a. Three hundred dollars
    b. Fifty dollars
    c. Four thousand dollars
    d. Forty thousand dollars

11. What did Dolly ask John to do with the money she and the Colonel won?
    a. To give it away to someone needy
    b. To put it in the bank for her
    c. To put it in his jeans pocket for safekeeping
    d. To share it with Lorraine

12. What did John ultimately do with the money the Colonel and Dolly won?
    a. He doubled the money at the blackjack table.
    b. He deposited it in a local bank.
    c. He shared it with Lorraine.
    d. He lost the money gambling.

Pigman's Legacy Multiple Choice Quizzes page 15

Chapter Twelve

1. Who finally told Dolly and the Colonel about their lost money?
    a. The local police
    b. John himself
    c. Lorraine
    d. Gus

2. After she got over her initial shock, how did Dolly respond to losing the money?
    a. She called the police.
    b. She slapped John.
    c. She said that it was all right and John shouldn't worry about it.
    d. She blamed Lorraine.

3. What was the Colonel's response when John and Lorraine offered to pay back his money by cleaning his house and bringing him food?
    a. He said that would work out fine.
    b. He said they didn't have to do that.
    c. He said that wasn't good enough.
    d. He said he would never forgive them for the loss of his money.

4. What present did the Colonel give to Dolly as they returned home from Atlantic City?
    a. A silver dollar
    b. His special medallion
    c. A huge diamond ring
    d. A pair of diamond earrings

5. What does Lorraine learn from watching how supportive Dolly is of the Colonel?
    a. That even old people can be in love
    b. That even someone like Dolly can find a boyfriend
    c. That Dolly was really stronger than she had seemed at first
    d. That she should be more supportive of John when he is troubled

6. What happened to the Colonel in the car returning from Atlantic City?
    a. He died.
    b. He vomited.
    c. He sang all the way home.
    d. He became very sick again.

Pigman's Legacy Multiple Choice Quizzes page 16

Chapters Thirteen and Fourteen

1. What did Dolly, John, and Lorraine do to help the Colonel when he got sick again?
    a. They fed him chicken soup.
    b. They tried to talk him into seeing a doctor.
    c. They took him to a hospital.
    d. They called for an ambulance.

2. What revelation does Dolly make about the Colonel's medical condition?
    a. That he is dying
    b. That he is faking his illness
    c. That he is really a hypochondriac
    d. That his only real medical problem is old age

3. What announcement does the Colonel make at the hospital?
    a. That he wants to marry Dolly
    b. That he wants his dog
    c. That he really isn't the Colonel after all
    d. That he really is John's grandfather

4. What request does the Colonel make at the hospital?
    a. He asks for a priest to marry him and Dolly.
    b. He asks John to take care of his dog.
    c. He asks John to take care of Lorraine and Dolly.
    d. He asks John to take care of his special medallion.

5. Why did John decide to take Gus along to the hospital?
    a. Because he knew Gus would want to see the Colonel one last time
    b. Because the dog was trying to throw himself through a window to get out and John was afraid he would be cut on the glass
    c. Because he got tired of hearing the dog bark
    d. Because Gus was really old and might die before they all returned home

6. What did Gus do when he found the Colonel at the hospital?
    a. He barked loudly only once.
    b. He whined.
    c. He licked the dead Colonel's face.
    d. He bit the nurse.

Pigman's Legacy Multiple Choice Quizzes page 17

7. What happened to Gus at the end of the book?
   a. He went to live on a big farm in the country.
   b. He went home with the Colonel.
   c. John and Lorraine took him home.
   d. Dolly decided that she would keep Gus with her.

8. What was on the floor of the hospital where Lorraine stopped the elevator?
   a. A big puddle of water
   b. A huge cross on the wall
   c. Many newborn babies
   d. A lot of very old patients

9. What does John say to Lorraine at the end of the book?
   a. "I don't think you handled yourself very well today."
   b. "I really had a swell time today."
   c. "Let's do it all over again tomorrow, Lorraine."
   d. "I want to spend my life with you."

10. What was the legacy of John and Lorraine's Pigman?
    a. Love
    b. Wariness
    c. Adolescent fixations
    d. Death

Key: Multiple Choice Quizzes - The Pigman's Legacy

The Promise and Chapters 1 & 2
1. b
2. d
3. b
4. b
5. b
6. c
7. a
8. b
9. d
10. b
11. a
12. d

Chapters 3 & 4
1. b
2. b
3. b
4. b
5. c
6. b
7. d
8. b
9. a
10. a

Chapter 5
1. b
2. b
3. b
4. d
5. c

Chapter 6
1. a
2. d
3. d
4. b
5. b
6. b
7. c
8. c
9. c
10. d
11. b
12. a

Chapters 7 & 8
1. c
2. d
3. b
4. b
5. d
6. b
7. b
8. b
9. a
10. d

Chapters 9-10
1. c
2. b
3. b
4. b
5. d
6. b
7. b
8. c
9. c
10. a

Chapter 11
1. d
2. d
3. d
4. b
5. c
6. a
7. a
8. b
9. a
10. c
11. c
12. d

Chapter 12
1. c
2. c
3. b
4. b
5. d
6. d

Chapters 13 & 14
1. c
2. a
3. a
4. a
5. b
6. c
7. d
8. c
9. d
10. a

VOCABULARY WORKSHEETS

Vocabulary - The Pigman's Legacy

<u>The Promise and Chapters One and Two</u> Part 1: Using Prior Knowledge and Contextual Clues. Below are the sentences in which the vocabulary words appear in the text. Read the sentence. Use any clues you can find in the sentence combined with your prior knowledge, and write what you think the underlined words mean

1. His name was the Pigman and certain persons who read that **memorial** epic said we knocked him off.

2. In case you didn't read the first memorial **epic** Lorraine and I wrote about the Pigman, don't worry about it.

3. The only practical jokes I do now are those designed to show the warm **foibles** of being human.

4. Also, I've given up writing **graffiti** on desks.

5. Also you should know I now don't **condone** the marking and destruction of public property.

6. Whenever I see these subway trains and buses with Magic Marker writing and spray-can painting on them, I'd like to get whoever did it and **immerse** them in a vat of two-hundred-year-old wonton soup.

7. I am not a **pubescent** expert on anything.

8. I simply happen to like **psychology** and read a lot of books on the subject.

9. Some people said we weren't **fleecing** him and that we weren't responsible for his death

10. We've already met our Pigman and can now tell you how we found out whether the **legacy** he left us was the legacy of life or the legacy of death.

11. It was last May, about four months after our Pigman died, that John and I were riding home **platonically** as usual after school….

12. And I told him that **sublimation** was just as dangerous as anything else the human mind could do….

13. A little old nun was sitting on top of a small tractor mower, cutting the grass in front of the Grymes Hill **Convent** there.

Pigman's Legacy The Promise and Chapters One and Two Vocabulary page 2

14. We did the best we could to muffle our giggles because we didn't want the nun to think we were laughing at her even though she was a bit of a sight sitting atop that tractor with her habit and the chopped grass **undulating** in the air behind her.

15. The bushes had grown so wild the house was **submerged** in a jungle of vines and thorns.

Part II: Determining the Meaning   Match the vocabulary words to their dictionary definitions.

___ 1. memorial   A. under, beneath
___ 2. epic   B. a monastic community or house, especially of nuns
___ 3. foibles   C. overlook; forgive; disregard
___ 4. graffiti   D. commemorating, serving as a reminder of
___ 5. condone   E. transcending physical desire; spiritual
___ 6. psychology   F. modifying natural expression or instinctual impulse
___ 7. immerse   G. literary work that suggests epic grandeur or heroics
___ 8. undulating   H. defrauding of money or property; swindling
___ 9. pubescent   I. science that deals with mental processes and behavior
___10. legacy   J. making a wavelike movement
___11. platonically   K. minor weaknesses or failings of character
___12. fleecing   L. reaching or having reached puberty
___13. submerged   M. drawing or inscription on wall or other surface
___14. sublimation   N. covered completely in something else
___15. convent   O. something handed down, as from an ancestor

Pigman's Legacy Vocabulary page 3 Chapters Three and Four

Part I: Using Prior Knowledge and Contextual Clues
Below are the sentences in which the vocabulary words appear in the text. Read the sentence. Use any clues you can find in the sentence combined with your prior knowledge, and write what you think the underlined words mean.

1. But the really weird part was that Dolly Racinski wore giant-sized pom-pom-shaped **rhinestone** earrings that sparkled exactly as if she was wearing flashlights in her ears.

2. She started quoting all these weird cases, like the time some famous poetess died and all her relatives saw this **apparition** rise up off her body and dance on the ceiling.

3. Lorraine's mother is still a **widow** and a practical nurse who steals things like Lipton Cup-a-Soup and skinless sardines from houses where she works...

4. His conversation is still so **stimulating** I continue to call him Bore.

5. It really takes the heat off us now that our parents, our teachers, and everybody knows that life is *all* **adolescence.**

6. The kind they call **poltergeists**.

7. "We'll be **trespassing**."

8. We couldn't turn the house into a **shrine** for the dead.

9. "Someone is here," he said with an assurance that made my jaw **petrify**.

10. And what happened next almost gave me a **thrombosis**.

Part II: Determining the Meaning   Match the vocabulary words to their dictionary definitions.

___ 16. rhinestone   A. formation of blood clot in a vessel or the heart
___ 17. apparition   B. period from puberty to maturity; teen years
___ 18. widow   C. site revered for its associations
___ 19. thrombosis   D. come to become stonelike; to deaden
___ 20. trespassing   E. a colorless artificial gem of paste or glass
___ 21. stimulating   F. a ghost
___ 22. adolescence   G. woman whose husband has died
___ 23. petrify   H. invading the property rights of another
___ 24. shrine   I. exciting

Pigman's Legacy Vocabulary page 4 Chapter Five

Part I: Using Prior Knowledge and Contextual Clues
Below are the sentences in which the vocabulary words appear in the text. Read the sentence. Use any clues you can find in the sentence combined with your prior knowledge, and write what you think the underlined words mean.

1. And the head itself was set upon a skinny and practically neckless **frail** body.

2. This **gruff** voice emerged from the old lips.

3. "I'm waiting for an answer!" his voice finally said in a **wheeze**.

4. "You mean '**squatting**' here," Lorraine corrected.

5. I could just see this **dossier** growing in her mind.

6. "Farewell, old house," I sadly mumbled as we ran out to the **dilapidated** porch and didn't stop before we hit the street.

7. "It's the Pigman," Lorraine said. "That man is the Pigman **reincarnated**."

8. Nobody answered, but that didn't come as a surprise, knowing that the old guy might be in a **stupor**.

Part II: Determining the Meaning   Match the vocabulary words to their dictionary definitions.

___ 25. frail   A. daze
___ 26. gruff   B. reborn
___ 27. squatting   C. in disrepair, deterioration, or ruin
___ 28. wheeze   D. not substantial; slight
___ 29. dossier   E. brief and unfriendly; harsh
___ 30. dilapidated   F. collection of papers about a particular person
___ 31. reincarnated   G. hoarse whistling sound
___ 32. stupor   H. settling without legal claim

Pigman's Legacy Vocabulary page 5 Chapter Six

Part I: Using Prior Knowledge and Contextual Clues
Below are the sentences in which the vocabulary words appear in the text. Read the sentence. Use any clues you can find in the sentence combined with your prior knowledge, and write what you think the underlined words mean.

33. It was very uncomfortable sitting totally across the room from the old guy and having him look at us as though we were **mannequins** in a department store.

34. "Yes, *you*," he said, fiddling now with the **medallion** around his neck.

35. John handed the **fossil** to me right away.

36. Finally I was able to read it aloud: *To the Colonel, for fifty years of service*, the **engraving** said.

37. "You should come to our high school some time and help Mrs. Stein teach a **geology** lesson."

38. And I'm not **naïve**.

Part II: Determining the Meaning   Match the vocabulary words to their dictionary definitions.

___ 33. mannequins   A. science of the origin, history, and structure of the earth
___ 34. medallion   B. simple; lacking worldliness and sophistication
___ 35. fossil   C. carved or etched into a surface
___ 36. engraved   D. a large medal
___ 37. geology   E. skeleton or leaf imprint
___ 38. naïve   F. dummies

Pigman's Legacy Vocabulary page 6 Chapters Seven and Eight

Part I: Using Prior Knowledge and Contextual Clues
Below are the sentences in which the vocabulary words appear in the text. Read the sentence. Use any clues you can find in the sentence combined with your prior knowledge, and write what you think the underlined words mean.

1. "I just had a **vision**," he said.

2. "John, I just know this is an **omen**." Lorraine said.

3. There was the town house, five stories of dark stone that looked like a private sanatorium for **indigent** berserk persons.

4. We thought it was best to let Gus have his little **reverie**, and then we could be on our way again.

5. It had a little gold plate underneath it that said it was a **stegosaurus**.

6. "I feel like I'm standing in a **mausoleum**," Lorraine said.

7. I never felt more **mortified** than when he made me help him drag the trunk down the outside steps while people were walking back and forth on the street.

Part II: Determining the Meaning   Match the vocabulary words to their dictionary definitions.

___ 39. vision   A. humiliated; shamed
___ 40. omen   B. experience of seeing the supernatural as if with the eyes
___ 41. reverie   C. a large stately tomb
___ 42. indigent   D. dinosaur with a double row of bony plates on its back
___ 43. Stegosaurus   E. a state of abstract musing
___ 44. mausoleum   F. sign of future good or evil
___ 45. mortified   G. impoverished; needy

Pigman's Legacy Vocabulary page 7   Chapters Nine and Ten

Part I: Using Prior Knowledge and Contextual Clues
Below are the sentences in which the vocabulary words appear in the text. Read the sentence. Use any clues you can find in the sentence combined with your prior knowledge, and write what you think the underlined words mean.

46. The Colonel couldn't talk, and you could see he was trying to hold back his **anguish**, but he still had to cry out in pain.

47. "Haven't you got **Medicare**?" the mean nurse pursued.

48. The Colonel hadn't paid real-estate taxes on the town house in years, and the only source of income we could find for him since he had retired was something called a **Keogh** Plan, where he was supposed to pay taxes on money which he himself had saved.

49. Lookin' up," she said **perkily**, "lookin' up!"

50. The force of her **conviction** caused her earrings to bounce against her cheeks.

51. It said if you could just remember that "A" stands for **abstinence**, "B" is for baby, and "C" is for contraception, then everything would work out all right in life.

Part II: Determining the Meaning   Match the vocabulary words to their dictionary definitions.

___ 46. anguish   A. deliberate restraining of oneself; not indulging
___ 47. Medicare   B. strong belief
___ 48. Keogh   C. in a lively way
___ 49. perkily   D. agonizing physical or mental pain
___ 50. conviction   E. government program for medical care for those over 65
___ 51. abstinence   F. retirement plan for the self-employed

Pigman's Legacy Vocabulary page 8 Chapter Eleven

Part I: Using Prior Knowledge and Contextual Clues
Below are the sentences in which the vocabulary words appear in the text. Read the sentence. Use any clues you can find in the sentence combined with your prior knowledge, and write what you think the underlined words mean.

1. Lorraine had borrowed a few of her mother's nursing journals, and she was **surreptitiously** flipping through those as a sort of handy reference guide in case the Colonel had another attack on the way.

2. And he didn't doze off again on the whole trip, which had to be due to Dolly's **vivaciousness**.

3. There was something about the new marble facade and the automatic doors with the electronic **surveillance** system that didn't go with the rest of the building.

4. It seemed like all of them were **zombies** even when their machines came up winners.

5. Dolly's **ecstasy** and her electric blue swirl dress caught everyone's attention.

6. It's like some **disciple** of the devil just grabbed my hand and thrust it into my left pocket to pull out the wad of C-notes.

Part II: Determining the Meaning   Match the vocabulary words to their dictionary definitions.

___ 52. surreptitiously   A. assistant; follower
___ 53. vivaciousness   B. delight
___ 54. surveillance   C. secretly
___ 55. zombies   D. close observation
___ 56. ecstasy   E. liveliness; spiritedness; animation
___ 57. disciple   F. people who look and behave like robots

Pigman's Legacy Vocabulary page 9 Chapter Twelve

Part I: Using Prior Knowledge and Contextual Clues
Below are the sentences in which the vocabulary words appear in the text. Read the sentence. Use any clues you can find in the sentence combined with your prior knowledge, and write what you think the underlined words mean.

58. When he didn't speak, I just **blurted** it out.

59. The retarded valet had stepped on the emergency brake so heavily that we couldn't release it until John **inverted** himself under the dashboard and yanked around at some wires and springs.

60. It's the people in this world who never try who go to their grave full of **regrets**.

61. The fumes from the Jersey **refineries** smacked us in our faces, and they smelled like death.

Part II: Determining the Meaning   Match the vocabulary words to their dictionary definitions.

___ 58. blurted   A. Plants that purify crude substances
___ 59. inverted   B. Feels sorry about
___ 60. regrets   C. Said
___ 61. refineries   D. Turned inside out or upside down

Pigman's Legacy Vocabulary   page 10   Chapter s Thirteen and Fourteen

Part I: Using Prior Knowledge and Contextual Clues
Below are the sentences in which the vocabulary words appear in the text. Read the sentence. Use any clues you can find in the sentence combined with your prior knowledge, and write what you think the underlined words mean.

1. Lorraine and I stood **mute** and helpless, and we were so grateful for having an adult help us for a change.

2. I guess we sensed the **limitations** of being a kid when the chips were down.

3. "*Serendipity*," I said, and it was the first time I had ever used the word in my life.

4. The Colonel's face **ignited** with joy.

5. And then I did something **instinctive**.

6. I was **mesmerized**, being drawn back through time and up into the highest, most brilliant galaxies.

Part II: Determining the Meaning   Match the vocabulary words to their dictionary definitions.

___ 62. mute   A. restrictions; boundaries
___ 63. limitations   B. lit up
___ 64. serendipity   C. silent; unable to speak
___ 65. ignited   D. impulsive
___ 66. instinctive   E. hypnotized
___ 67. mesmerized   F. ability to make fortunate discoveries by accident

Key: Vocabulary Worksheets - The Pigman's Legacy

1. D	18. G	35. E	52. C
2. G	19. A	36. C	53. E
3. K	20. H	37. A	54. D
4. M	21. I	38. B	55. F
5. C	22. B	39. B	56. B
6. I	23. D	40. F	57. A
7. N	24. C	41. E	58. C
8. J	25. D	42. G	59. D
9. L	26. E	43. D	60. B
10. O	27. H	44. C	61. A
11. E	28. G	45. A	62. C
12. H	29. F	46. D	63. A
13. A	30. C	47. E	64. F
14. F	31. B	48. F	65. B
15. B	32. A	49. C	66. D
16. E	33. F	50. B	67. E
17. F	34. D	51. A	

DAILY LESSON PLANS

Lesson One

Objectives
1. To introduce the unit on **The Pigman's Legacy**
2. To distribute books and other related materials (study guides, reading assignments, etc.)
3. To preview the study questions for The Promise (introduction) and Chapters One and Two
4. To familiarize students with the vocabulary for The Promise and Chapters One and Two
5. To begin consideration and discussion of one theme in **The Pigman's Legacy**, namely sharing with others and leaving a legacy

NOTE: Prior to this lesson, students should have been assigned to bring in the item they own that they most value (or a written physical description, photograph, or drawing of that item). Borrowing from the situation in **The Pigman's Legacy** in which the Colonel gives his cherished medallion to Dolly Racinski, students should be encouraged to think about what they have that would mean as much as the Colonel's medallion to give away to someone they love. You will have prepared ahead of time a bulletin board that has the title MY LEGACY: THE BEST I HAVE TO GIVE. You may want to place pictures on the board. Remember to include pictures of both tangible and intangible things. For instance, you might have some valuable possessions pictured but will also want to show pictures of people embracing, people getting medical checkups, people in school, people in religious setting, etc. The point, of course, is that our most cherished possessions might include good health, a spiritual relationship, and friendship as well as the things we own.

Activity #1
Ask students individually to explain the significance to them of their most valuable possession. If they can, they might also explain who they would give the item to if they were giving it away. After they have explained this, each student should go to the bulletin board and either write a few words to describe their chosen item or, if they have a picture, post a picture of the item on the board. Students should be encouraged to keep all valuables with them and not leave them lying around in the classroom.

Activity #2
Distribute the materials students will use in this unit. Explain in detail how students are to use the materials.

Study Guides Students should read the study guide questions for each reading assignment before beginning the assignment to get a feeling for what events and ideas are important in the section they are about to read. After reading the section, students will (as a class or individually) answer the questions to review the important events and ideas from that section of the book. Students should keep the study guides as study materials for the unit test.

Lesson One continued page 2

Vocabulary As they are reading a section of the text, students will do vocabulary work related to the section they are reading. If they hunt for the vocabulary words as they read, students should be able to figure out the contextual meaning of the words. Following the completion of the reading of the book, there will be a vocabulary review of all the words used in the vocabulary assignments. Students should keep their vocabulary work as study materials for the unit test.

Reading Assignment Sheet   You need to fill in the reading assignment sheet to let students know when their reading has to be completed. You can either write the assignment on a side black board or bulletin board and leave it there for students to see each day, or you can make copies for each student to have. In any case, advise students to become very familiar with the reading assignments so they know what is expected of them.

Extra Activities Center   The Extra Activities Packet portion of this unit contains suggestions for a library of related books and articles in your classroom as well as crossword and word search puzzles. Make a center in your room where you will keep these materials for students to use. (Bring the books and articles in from the library and keep several copies of the puzzles on hand.) Explain to students that these materials are available for their use when they finish reading assignments or other class work early.

Nonfiction Assignment Sheet Explain to students that they each are to read at least one nonfiction piece from the in-class library at some time during the unit. Students will fill out a nonfiction assignment sheet after completing the reading to help you evaluate their reading experiences and to help the students to think about and evaluate their own reading.

Books Each school has its own rules and regulations regarding student use of school books. Advise students of the procedures that are usual for your school.

Activity #3
Preview the study questions and have students look over the vocabulary words for The Promise and Chapters One and Two of **The Pigman's Legacy**. If students do not finish this assignment during the class period, they should complete it, including the vocabulary worksheets, prior to the next class meeting

NONFICTION ASSIGNMENT SHEET - The Pigman's Legacy
(To be completed after reading the required nonfiction article)

Name _____ Date _____ Class _____

Title of Nonfiction Read _____

Author _____ Publication Date _____

I. **Factual Summary**: Write a short summary of the piece you read.

II. **Vocabulary**:
    1. Which vocabulary words were difficult?

    2. What did you do to help yourself understand the words?

III. **Interpretation**: What was the main point the author wanted you to get from reading his or her work?

IV. **Criticism**:
    1. Which points of the piece did you agree with or find easy to believe? Why?

    2. Which points did you disagree with or find hard to believe? Why?

V. **Personal Response**:
    1. What do you think about this piece?

    2. How does this piece help you better understand the book **The Pigman's Legacy**?

Oral Reading Evaluation - The Pigman's Legacy

Name _____ Class _____ Date _____

SKILL	EXCELLENT	GOOD	AVERAGE	FAIR	POOR
Fluency	5	4	3	2	1
Clarity	5	4	3	2	1
Audibility	5	4	3	2	1
Pronunciation	5	4	3	2	1
_____	5	4	3	2	1
_____	5	4	3	2	1

Total _____ Grade _____

Comments:

Lesson Two

Objectives
1. To read the introduction (The Promise) and Chapters One and Two
2. To give students practice reading orally
3. To evaluate students' oral reading
4. To preview the study questions for Chapters Three and Four
5. To do the pre-reading vocabulary work for Chapters Three and Four

Activity

Have students read The Promise and Chapters One and Two of **The Pigman's Legacy** out loud in class. You probably know the best way to choose readers from your class: pick students at random, ask for volunteers, or use whatever other method works best for your group. If you have not yet completed an oral reading evaluation for your students this marking period, this would be a good opportunity to do so. A form is included with this unit for your convenience.

If students do not complete reading through Chapter Two in class, they should do so prior to your next class meeting.

Also, tell students that prior to the next class meeting, they should have previewed the study questions and done the vocabulary worksheets for Chapters Three and Four.

Lesson Three

Objectives
1. To review the main events and ideas from the introduction and Chapters One and Two
2. To read Chapters Three and Four
3. To do the pre-reading and reading work for Chapter Five
4. To give students the opportunity to write to express a personal opinion

Activity #1

Give students a few minutes to formulate answers for the study guide questions through Chapter Two and then discuss the answers to the questions in detail. Each time you review the main events and ideas in a section of the book, you can use the short answer questions to guide the discussion. Then use the multiple choice quizzes when suggested in the unit guidelines or at any time that you think they will be useful to the students. For the short answers, write them on the board or overhead transparency so students can have the correct answers for study purposes. Note: It is a good practice in public speaking and leadership skills for individual students to take charge of leading the discussions of the study questions. Perhaps a different student could go to the front of the class and lead the discussion each day that the study questions are discussed during this unit. You will still guide the discussion when appropriate and be sure to fill in any gaps the students leave.

Lesson Three continued page 2

Activity #2

Have students read Chapters Three and Four of **The Pigman's Legacy** out loud in class. Use the method of selecting student readers that works best for you. Continue the oral reading evaluations.

Activity #3

Tell students that prior to the next class, they should have completed the pre-reading and reading work for Chapter Five. (Give students a specific day by which this assignment must be done.)

Activity #4

Have students complete Writing Assignment #2 (Writing to Express a Personal Opinion). The directions for the assignment follow.

Writing Assignment #1 - The Pigman's Legacy
(Writing to Express a Personal Opinion)

PROMPT
It is clear early in the book that John and Lorraine are becoming romantically attracted to each other. They write secret passages in the book about how they are or are not romantically involved. Lorraine says that they talk platonically, but she makes a big point of explaining how she likes to hold John's hand and walk alone with him. But the two characters are sixteen years old. The question is, is it possible for two people to love each other deeply and lastingly when they are sixteen? Your assignment is write a composition in which you express your personal opinion about whether true love is possible at age sixteen.

PREWRITING
Think about what you know personally about love, what you have observed about people in love, and perhaps what you have read about love. Think about whether it is possible to have a real loving relationship with a person when you both are sixteen. Think, for example, if it is possible for a couple to fall in love at sixteen and then be together for the rest of their lives and remain in love with each other.

DRAFTING
Write an introductory paragraph in which you state that you have been asked your opinion about whether it is possible to really be in love at sixteen. Then state your opinion about whether or not it is possible and give three reasons to back up your opinion.

Write at least one paragraph explaining and supporting each of your reasons. Make sure that you give the reader all of the information needed to understand your point of view fully.

Write a concluding paragraph in which you summarize what you have said in the essay .

PROMPT
When you finish the rough draft of your paper, ask a student who sits near you to read it. The other student is not reading it to see if he or she agrees or disagrees with your main point but only to see if your main point is clearly and convincingly expressed. After reading your rough draft, he or she should tell you what he or she liked best about your work, which parts were difficult to understand, and ways in which your work could be improved. Reread your paper considering your critic's comments and make the corrections you think are necessary.

PROOFREADING
Do a final proofreading of your paper, double-checking your grammar, spelling, organization, and the clarity of your ideas.

Lesson Four

Objectives
1. To review the main events and ideas from Chapters Three, Four, and Five
2. To do the pre-reading work for Chapter Six
3. To remind students to read Chapter Six before the next class
4. To give students the opportunity to examine and discuss language and usage using **The Pigman's Legacy** as a starting point

Activity #1
Take some time to be sure that students are following the action of **The Pigman's Legacy** and that they understand the main ideas presented in the book so far.

Activity #2
Give students some time individually or in small groups to do the pre-reading work for Chapter Six.

Activity #3
Both of the teenagers who tell the story of **The Pigman's Legacy** have interesting writing styles. John tends to use colloquial language and to make jokes whenever possible. Lorraine tends to use a pseudo sophisticated language that may result from her interest in the field of psychology. Both of the writers are romantics in their own ways, and because they are good friends, they pick up on ideas in each other's chapters and sometimes needle each other a little about what has been said. Thus we encounter colloquial words and terms like *knocked him off*, *stuff*, *barf*, and *boys' john*, but we also need to check our dictionaries from time to time to check terms like *pubescent*, *sublimation*, and *undulating*.

When John calls Lorraine a *kind of pubescent expert on psychology*, she immediately disclaims such a title. Both teenagers type "secret" paragraphs in their chapters that are, of course, discovered by the other. Both are more than a little bit in love with the other.

You may use this information in any way that you please. One way is to look at the impact of various types of words and phrases. Invite students to look at the differences between *regurgitate*, *vomit*, *throw up*, and *barf*. Try to get them to discuss the implications of terms such as *killed*, *murdered*, and *knocked off*. This might be a good time to introduce terms such as *connotation*, *denotation*, *euphemism*, and *politically correct phrases*. It might be fun to concoct a list of terms to look at and discuss in small groups. You are well advised not to become the arbiter of language during this exercise. Try instead to guide students to think about levels of usage rather than to judge them.

If you like, you may use the little exercise on language that follows. Encourage students to have fun with the exercise.

Activity #4
Remind students that they should read Chapter Six before the next class period.

Exercise on Language and Levels of Usage
The Pigman's Legacy

One of the most interesting ways to investigate language usage is to think about and discuss the impact that different levels of usage have on others. Think about the difference between raising your hand and telling the teacher, "I need to leave the room because I think I'm going to be sick" or saying, "I gotta split 'cause I'm gonna barf." Think about a death in the family of a friend. Do you say, "Sorry about your grandmother's passing away" or do you blurt out, "Sorry your grandmother kicked the bucket"?

Here are a few terms that might be useful to you in considering usage.

Denotation usually refers to the actual dictionary definition. **Connotation**, on the other hand, usually refers to what the word implies, the images or associations it evokes in people. A **euphemism** is a polite, sometimes evasive, way of saying something. Often today we use a lot of euphemisms in order to be sure our speech is **politically correct**. Sometimes politically correct phrases seem exaggerated in order to avoid any potential offense to anyone who might hear them.

Let's look at a single idea. Someone who is **dead** is no longer alive. So we can say that a person got very sick and **died**. When we are joking around, we might suggest that someone has **croaked** or **kicked the bucket**. Euphemistically we can, and often do, say that the person is **deceased** or has **passed, passed on, gone to his reward, gone to heaven,** or **gone to be with God.** Various cultures use forms of these terms to avoid the pain and discomfort of talking directly about death. In terms of political correctness, we would no doubt be reduced to saying that the person is **life challenged**.

Language is never good or bad, only appropriate or inappropriate. Someone who has **passed away** is just as dead as the person who has **croaked**. The person who **is downsized** is just as out of work as the person who is **fired**. The person who is **sight deprived** is just as unable to see as the person who is **blind**. But sometimes one term might be much more preferable than another as we try to be socially acceptable, to save people hurt and grief, to give all people the dignity they deserve, and to explain our personal feelings about the subject we are discussing.

Look at the list of words that can be used to describe someone who has had too much to drink. Discuss in your small group the different levels of meaning for each term. Discuss which terms would be appropriate and inappropriate under specific conditions.

intoxicated
inebriated
drunk
in one's cups
smashed

DWI
under the influence
sloshed
sobriety challenged
hitting the bottle
off the wagon
out of it
wasted
has a buzz on

Then go on to discuss terms for other situations. What do we call people who speed while driving their cars? People who are not intelligent? People who are not physically attractive? Fat people? Skinny people? How about people who are not good with computers? People who get good grades? Ideas that are very good? Ideas that are not good? What do people call you when they are being unpleasant? When they are being polite?

Have fun with this exercise, but remember that words are very powerful. Learn to use them knowingly and carefully. Say what you mean and be as direct as possible, but don't go out of your way to put others at a disadvantage or to make yourself seem callous toward another person or group of people. In some areas of the country, it is just plain wrong to use certain phrases to describe people and situations. Learn what is appropriate and inappropriate in your area and then decide accordingly how you wish to speak.

Lesson Five

Objectives
1. To review Chapter Six
2. To do the preview work for Chapters Seven and Eight
3. To give students the opportunity to write to inform/explain
4. To assign the reading for Chapters Seven and Eight

Activity #1

Spend some time reviewing the main events and ideas in Chapters Five and Six. Be sure that all of the students are keeping up with their reading and are understanding the story line.

Activity #2

Give students a brief time to do the preview work for Chapters Seven and Eight.

Activity #3

Have students write during class. Their essay will be based on their explaining their version of the Colonel's Game of Life. A sheet of directions follows.

Activity #4

Remind students that they are supposed to have read Chapters Seven and Eight prior to the next class meeting.

Writing Assignment #2 - The Pigman's Legacy
(Writing to Inform/Explain)

PROMPT
In **The Pigman's Legacy**, the Colonel has John close his eyes and envision a variety of things in order to play The Game of Life. As John envisions the road, key, cup, tree, and wall, the Colonel interprets what the items mean in John's life. This game, the Colonel, says, is the only one he knows.

Your assignment is to envision your own Game of Life. Although the Colonel includes five different items, you need only think of three. Your assignment is to write a composition in which you explain to someone else what three items would be found in your Game of Life and what your three items would be like. Be sure to describe the items in as much detail as possible. Refer back to Chapter Six of **The Pigman's Legacy** if you need to review the Colonel's Game of Life explanation.

PRE-WRITING
Think through what you think your Game of Life should be like and what three items would be included in it. Then try to decide what the three items in your particular Game of Life would be like if you were describing them as John did to the Colonel.

DRAFTING
Write an introductory paragraph in which you introduce your Game of Life. You might tell in the first paragraph whether your Game is easy or hard to play. Then you might mention the three items that are in your Game. In the body of the composition, explain each of the three items as they would be found were you personally playing the Game. And, finally, write a concluding paragraph in which you explain what has been learned in the rest of the paper.

PROMPT
When you finish the rough draft of your paper, ask a student who sits near you to read it. After reading your rough draft, he or she should tell you what he or she liked best about your work, which parts were difficult to understand, and ways in which your work could be improved. Reread your paper considering your critic's comments, and make the corrections you think are necessary.

PROOFREADING
Do a final proofreading of your paper, double checking your grammar, spelling , organization, and the clarity of your ideas.

Lesson Six

Objectives
1. To review the main events and ideas in Chapters Seven and Eight
2. To do the preview work for Chapters Nine and Ten
3. To read Chapters Nine and Ten
4. To prepare students for the library work on the nonfiction reading assignment

Activity #1
Review the main events and ideas in Chapters Seven and Eight. Be sure to take any questions that students may have at this point in their reading.

Activity #2
Give students time in class to do the preview work for Chapters Nine and Ten.

Activity #3
Read Chapters Nine and Ten. If you have not had an opportunity to evaluate each student's reading, this would be a good time to do that using one of the Oral Reading Evaluation forms for each student.

Activity #4
Hand out a list of possible topics on which students may read and report for their Nonfiction Reading Assignment. Check to see if there are any questions regarding the choices of topics.

Lesson Seven

Objective
To give students the opportunity to choose a nonfiction assignment topic, to read on that topic, and to fill out the Nonfiction Reading Assignment sheet for the reading that they do.

Activity
Students can meet in the library for this class, or they can meet in your regular classroom for some background information on the assignment and then proceed to the library together. Explain to students the purpose of their doing a nonfiction reading assignment. See if they have questions about their topics. Invite students to choose topics other than those listed as potential choices but to do so (1) only if they have thought through the idea and have a good reason for wanting to read about it, and (2) only if they have discussed their topic choice with you.

Explain the Nonfiction Reading Assignment sheet and make sure students know how to complete it.

Topics to Choose for Nonfiction Reading Assignment
The Pigman's Legacy

You may choose any of the following topics for your Nonfiction Reading Assignment. All of the topics are based in some way on **The Pigman's Legacy**. If you wish to read about some other topics, you must clear it with your teacher *before you begin the assignment*.

1. The Internal Revenue Service (IRS)
   (how it originated, what its purpose is, its relationship to the citizenry, abuses of power, structure of, differences over the years, who is in charge of it, what happens to people who refuse to pay their taxes, etc.)

2. The Elderly
   (programs to support the elderly, nursing homes, retirement communities, age to which people are now living, old age in America, old age in other cultures, medical problems of old age, medical services for older citizens, exercise and strength building, etc.)

3. Smoking
   (legislation to curb smoking, the tobacco lobby, states dependent on growing tobacco, young people starting smoking, diseases related to smoking, costs of smoking, problems of quitting smoking, alternatives to tobacco cigarettes, advertising connected to smoking, smoking in movies and/or on television, etc.)

4. Childhood
   (value of reading to children, child abuse, child care, surrogate parents, single-parent households, older women having children, adoption, foster care, books and/or movies for children, fantasies connected to childhood, etc.)

5. Graffiti
   (problems of graffiti, cost of removing, values of, cities where it is prevalent, etc.)

6. Reincarnation
   (what it is, does it really exist?, etc.)

7. Friendship
   (great friendships through the years, unusual friendships, friendships that came about during wars, etc.)

8. Parent/Child Relationships
   (parent/child relationships at various ages, relationships between parents and children in other cultures, etc.)

Topics for Nonfiction Reading Assignment continued page 2

9. Adolescence
(problems related to, what it means, its effect on the economy, society's view of, etc.)

10. Dogs as Pets
(keeping dogs in large cities, dog licensure, ways to find lost pets, German shepherds and their qualities, resource dogs, seeing eye dogs, rescue dogs, dog training, dogs kept for protection, laws regarding dogs, etc.)

Lesson Eight

Objectives
1. To review the main events and ideas in Chapters Nine and Ten
2. To do the preview work for Chapter Eleven
3. To set up the parameters for Project Aging
4. To read Chapter Eleven

Activity #1
Review the main ideas and events in Chapters Nine and Ten.

Activity #2
Introduce Project Aging to your students (details included).

Activity #3
Remind students that they are to have read Chapter Eleven by the next class meeting.

PROJECT AGING

Objectives

Project Aging is a total class project for use in conjunction with the book **The Pigman's Legacy** by Paul Zindel. Since one of the main ideas in the book deals with the problems faced by an older man (the Colonel) as he tries to cope on his own, this is a good opportunity to acquaint students with the resources and facilities for the aging in your town. Although we hear about the elderly on television and in newspapers a lot, it is difficult for young people to grasp the magnitude of the new challenges presented by a rapidly aging American population. This project is a way to make your students aware of the fact that people are living longer and longer and are requiring many more social programs, housing, medical care, etc. than ever before.

You no doubt have a retirement community and probably a nursing center in your area that students can use as part of their project. Most communities for aging citizens will be welcome to help to educate students in return for some volunteer efforts on the students' part.

THE PROJECT

This project is separate from the rest of the unit on **The Pigman's Legacy,** so you can either use it while you are reading and reviewing the book or as a separate mini-unit after you have completed the unit tests for **The Pigman's Legacy**. Also, having it as a separate project enables you to either eliminate it or to use it, without disturbing the flow of the unit as a whole.

Assignment #1

Your local television station or newspaper should have some reports/articles on aging citizens in your area. Should you live in a small community that has fewer facilities of its own, you might want to focus on a metropolitan area nearby. Find several reports/articles on the aging population and show them to your students. Try to present the situation of older people in both positive and negative ways. Use the reports and articles as a springboard for a discussion of the challenges presented by a rapidly aging population.

Assignment #2

As a class, write a letter requesting the director of your local retirement community or nursing center to come to your class to discuss the concerns of the elderly. You may even have a facility nearby that includes a nursing center within a retirement community. Send the letter and then make any necessary follow-up phone calls to make arrangements for the visit.

Assignment #3

After students have the information you gather on aging, send them to the library to do some research. Each student should be able to read and summarize at least two articles on the topic. Hint: They might want to read about the average age of people in the retirement community, costs involved, benefits offered, what is available at the facilities, whether it is a multi-tiered

Project Aging continued page 2

facility offering assisted living and nursing care, what makes residents want to move there, what the facility's volunteer program is like, etc.

Assignment #4
After students have done their research, have them give oral reports about the articles they have read so that all students are exposed to the wealth of information that has been collectively read.

Assignment #5
Host the person who was invited to class in Assignment #2. This assignment should be done prior to undertaking Assignment #6.

Assignment #6
Divide students into groups of five or six. Explain that their job is to make a list of concerns of the elderly and to brainstorm ways that those concerns could be addressed in your town.

Students might focus, for example, on preparing early in life for a long old age, adjusting fees so that more people would be able to live comfortably as they age, developing or improving available volunteer programs that assist older people even while they remain on their own. They might want to look at some church groups that drive older people to and from doctors' appointments, help them to get their prescriptions, take them out shopping and to dinner, etc.

Appropriate class time will need to be spent on this brainstorming.

After the brainstorming has been done, have each student focus on one way that he or she can address one issue presented by the elderly. The way that each students chooses should involve some amount of community involvement (letter writing, discussion groups, personal volunteerism, articles in the newspaper, having speakers talk at all local schools, other educational campaigns, etc.)

Assignment #7
Actually visit a retirement facility with your class. If you have not already had someone visit your class to speak, perhaps you could combine a visit to a retirement facility with an opportunity to ask questions of someone knowledgeable there.

Assignment #8
Have students follow through on their ideas for ways to address the concerns of the elderly. If they have chosen letter writing, for example, have them actually write the letters. If they think that more people should personally volunteer to help, then they could volunteer perhaps one day every other week at the retirement facility. If they think that an educational program would be useful, have them design the program. You might want to use some class time to allow students to update the rest of the

class on what steps they are taking. Sometimes the other students may be able to make suggestions and criticisms that will be helpful in carrying out the project.

Assignment #9

After the project is finished, have a short wrap-up to allow students to discuss the value of the project overall. Try to get students to articulate what they learned from participating in the project. See if they will do anything differently in the future as a result of the knowledge they have gained. See if they think that their involvement has made any improvement in the situations that they investigated.

Lesson Nine

Objectives
1. To do the preview work for Chapter Twelve
2. To read Chapter Twelve
3. To review the main ideas, events, and characterizations in the book through Chapter Twelve

Activity #1
Give students a short period of time to do the preview work for Chapter Twelve. This far into the unit, this sort of work should be completed rather quickly.

Activity #2
Read Chapter Twelve as quickly as possible. It is a relatively short chapter.

Activity #3
Spend the rest of the class period reviewing the main ideas, events, and characterizations in the book through Chapter Twelve. Try to see that students have a clear idea of the personalities and motivations of John, Lorraine, Dolly, and the Colonel. If time allows, encourage students to think about the personalities and motivations of minor characters as well, such as the nurse on duty at the hospital when John and Lorraine took the Colonel in, the valets in Atlantic City, and even John and Lorraine's parents, although they never actually appear as characters in the book.

Ask students to spend some time between classes thinking about the characters in the book. Encourage them to try to better understand the characters by putting them into different contexts. For example, have students think about bringing one or more of the characters home with them. Tell students to think about how John, Lorraine, Dolly, and the Colonel would react in the new setting of the students' homes. To understand the characters on a much more personal level, students should imagine them having at least one conversation with their parents or their siblings or friends.

Lesson Ten

Objective
To get students to understand the characters in **The Pigman's Legacy** better by envisioning them in different contexts.

Activity
Try to put aside one entire class to achieve this objective. What you are going to do is ask some of your students to do some role playing in front of the rest of the class. Because not everyone will have the opportunity to play a role in class, the other students will learn from observing. Both actors and observers should be encouraged to think about how the characters are going to act in each scenario.

Lesson Ten continued page 2

You will be the best judge of which students can be relied on to carry out the assignment with a reasonable degree of understanding and comfort.

Don't worry that you don't have enough time to accommodate this kind of role playing. Its object is not to rehearse or spend a lot of time preparing for the role playing. It is, instead, to think through very quickly how a character will act based on what students already know about them.

This activity will work best if you try to prepare the students to have a good time doing it. Make sure they realize that there is no totally right or totally wrong way to do the activity. Instead, they should listen closely to the scenarios that you lay out, think very quickly about how their assigned character would react to each, and then pretend to *be* that character to the best of their ability.

Choose the scenarios that you think your students will best understand. You may do one or two scenarios or all five. If you want, you can even make up new scenarios, with or without your students' help. Again, there is no right or wrong here. You are just moving the characters around a little bit in order to let students look at them a little differently and understand them a little bit better.

Read the scenario. Give students three to five minutes to prepare, and then give them five minutes to act out the scenario. The ONLY requirement is that students try as hard as possible to keep the character as he or she behaved in the book.

Scenario #1 Two students: Dolly Racinski and a younger student
Dolly Racinski has decided to go back to school and get her high school diploma. She has done her first writing assignment and has given it to another student to read over. The other student sees that Dolly's writing has some flaws but is afraid of being rude to a person old enough to be her grandmother. Dolly, for her part, wants desperately to learn and to improve but has no idea that she has trouble expressing herself in writing. After all, she thinks, she has no problem talking. ***Have the younger student critique Dolly's paper honestly.***

Scenario #2: John and Lorraine
Lorraine's mother has decided that it is not good for Lorraine to see John anymore outside of school. Thus she has told Lorraine that she is not to see John except during school hours. Lorraine now has to talk with John about her mother's decision. ***Have Lorraine explain her mother's decision to John and then have John and Lorraine decide how to proceed in the future.***

Scenario #3: The Colonel and Dolly
John's parents have invited the Colonel and Dolly to come to dinner at their house. The Colonel and Dolly know nothing about John's parents except what John has written in **The Pigman's Legacy**. Their biggest fear is how they will be accepted by the parents.

Lesson Ten continued page 3

They have to talk about whether or not they should accept the invitation. *Have the Colonel and Dolly talk about whether or not to accept the invitation and come to some agreement between them.*

Scenario #4: Lorraine and Dolly
Having seen how Dolly talks to the Colonel, Lorraine decides that she could learn some techniques about how to talk to a man she really likes. So far Lorraine feels that she has been unable to explain to John how much he means to her. Lorraine asks Dolly for her help. Dolly doesn't think she has any real expertise because she is, after all, just being herself. She doesn't see that there is any technique to her behavior. *Have Lorraine ask Dolly for advice and have Dolly respond to her request.*

Scenario #5: John and the Colonel
Having seen how Dolly treats the Colonel, John decides that the Colonel must have some special techniques for getting women to like him especially well. So far John feels that he has been unable to explain to Lorraine how much she means to him. John asks the Colonel for his help. The Colonel feels he has no real expertise because he is, after all, just as surprised as anybody that Dolly likes him. He doesn't think there is any technique involved at all. *Have John ask the Colonel for advice and have the Colonel respond to his request.*

Lesson Eleven

Objectives
1. To do the preview work for Chapters Thirteen and Fourteen
2. To read Chapters Thirteen and Fourteen

Activity #1
Allow students time enough to do the preview work for Chapters Thirteen and Fourteen.

Activity #2
Have students read Chapters Thirteen and Fourteen aloud in class. If you have not already evaluated their oral reading skills, this will be your last easily available opportunity to do so. Use the Oral Reading Evaluation form presented earlier in this unit.

Lesson Twelve

Objectives
1. To review all of the chapters of the book, allowing students to ask questions if they have any
2. To allow students to give updates on their project if you have chosen to do Project Aging, *or* To allow students to test their knowledge of **The Pigman's Legacy**
3. To allow students the opportunity to write to persuade

Activity #1
Spend enough time in class reviewing all of the chapters of the book to be sure that all of the students have read and understood the book. You might have an interesting discussion about whether or not the Pigman should have died in the end of the book. Students surely will have varying opinions about that.

Activity #2
Spend some time allowing students to update the rest of the class on their projects, or select a variety of multiple choice quizzes and give students a quiz on **The Pigman's Legacy**.

Activity #3
Have students complete Writing Assignment #3 (Writing to Persuade). Use the directions that follow in this unit.

Writing Assignment #3 - The Pigman's Legacy
(Writing to Persuade)

PROMPT

Now that you have finished reading and discussing The Pigman's Legacy in its entirely, you have no doubt formed some opinions about it. What you are going to do now is to write to persuade. In order to do that, you need to choose an argument to make. Pick one of the following topics. You will be arguing strongly pro or con:

1. Lorraine Jensen is a very believable (or unbelievable) character.
2. The Colonel should (or should not) have died at the end of the book.
3. The author of **The Pigman's Legacy** does (or does not) know a lot about teenagers.
4. **The Pigman's Legacy** is (or is not) suitable for a reader at my age level.
5. **The Pigman's Legacy** is a book about life (or about death).

PREWRITING

Choose your topic and decide which way you which to argue the issue. Make sure that you choose a point of view that you believe in. By brainstorming, make a list of all of the reasons you believe as you do. Then try to combine any of the reasons into groups of reasons. Then choose your three strongest points.

DRAFTING

Write an introductory paragraph in which you state as firmly as possible your argument. After reading your introductory paragraph, a reader should know exactly where you stand on the issue being discussed.

Then write one paragraph explaining each of your reasons. Make sure that you have explained your reasons thoroughly enough that you don't leave lots of questions in the mind of the reader. Write as forcefully as possible throughout.

Write a concluding paragraph in which you summarize your main points and conclude your argument.

PROMPT

When you finish the rough draft of your paper, ask a student who sits near you to read it. You want to know if you have argued your point well, not whether the other student necessarily agrees with your point. After reading your rough draft, he or she should tell you what he or she liked best about your work, which parts were difficult to understand, and ways in which your work could be improved. Reread your paper considering your critic's comments and make the corrections you think are necessary.

PROOFREADING

Do a final proofreading of your paper, double checking your grammar, spelling, organization, and the clarity of your ideas.

Lesson Thirteen

Objective
 To review the vocabulary work done in this unit

Activity

Choose one or more of the vocabulary review activities listed on the next page and spend your class period as directed in the activity. Some of the materials for these review activities are located in the Vocabulary Resource Materials at the end of this unit.

Vocabulary Review Activities

1. Divide your class into two teams and have an old-fashioned spelling or definition bee.

2. Give each of your students (or students in groups of two, three, or four) a Vocabulary Word Search Puzzle based on **The Pigman's Legacy**. The person or group to find all of the vocabulary words in the puzzle first wins.

3. Give students a **The Pigman's Legacy** Vocabulary Word Search Puzzle without the word list. The person or group to find the most vocabulary words in the puzzle wins.

4. Use a **The Pigman's Legacy** Vocabulary Crossword Puzzle. Put a puzzle onto a transparency on the overhead projector so everyone can see it and do the puzzle together as a class.

5. Give students a **The Pigman's Legacy** Vocabulary Matching Worksheet to do.

6. Divide your class into two teams. Use **The Pigman's Legacy** vocabulary words with their letters jumbled as a word list. Student 1 from Team A faces off against Student 1 from Team B. You write the first jumbled word on the board. The first student (1A or 1B) to unscramble the word wins the chance for his or her team to score points. If 1A wins the jumble, go to student 2A and give him or her a definition. He or she must give you the correct spelling of the vocabulary word which fits that definition. If he or she does, Team A scores a point, and you give student 3A a definition for which you expect a correctly spelled matching vocabulary word. Continue giving Team A definitions until some team member makes an incorrect response. An incorrect response sends the game back to the jumbled-word face off, this time with students 2A and 2B. Instead of repeating giving definitions to the first few students of each team, continue with the student after the one who gave the last incorrect response on the team. For example, if Team B wins the jumbled-word face-off and student 5B gave the last incorrect answer for Team B, you would start this round of definition questions with student 5B and so on. The team with the most points wins!

7. Have students write a story in which they correctly use as many vocabulary words as possible. Have students read their compositions orally! Post the most original compositions on your bulletin board.

Lesson Fourteen

Objectives
1. To discuss the ideas and themes from **The Pigman's Legacy** in greater detail
2. To have students exercise their critical thinking skills
3. To try to relate some of the ideas of **The Pigman's Legacy** to the students' lives

Activity #1
Choose the questions from the Extra Discussion Questions/Writing Assignments which seem most appropriate for your students. A class discussion of these questions is most effective if students have been given the opportunity to formulate answers to the questions prior to the discussion. To this end, you may either have all the students formulate answers to all the questions, divide your class into groups and assign one or more questions to each group, or assign one question to each student in your class. The option you choose will make a difference in the amount of time needed for this activity.

Activity #2
After students have had ample time to formulate answers to the questions, begin your class discussion of the questions and the ideas presented by the questions. Be sure students take notes during the discussion so they have information to study for the unit tests.

Extra Discussion Questions/Writing Assignments
The Pigman's Legacy

Interpretive
1. How is the retelling of the story structured, and why is it important that it is told that way?

2. Do a complete character analysis of any of the four major characters in the book.

3. What are the main conflicts in the book and how are they resolved?

4. What are the highest and lowest points of the book?

5. Does the reader know ahead of time basically how the book will end? Explain why or why not.

6. John uses a lot of colloquial expressions in his writing. How does this influence the reader's view of John?

Critical
1. What is the significance of the title, **The Pigman's Legacy**?

2, Compare and contrast the Colonel and Dolly Racinski.

3. Are the characters in **The Pigman's Legacy** believable or not? Explain why or why not.

4. Is the plot of **The Pigman's Legacy** realistic? Could a story like John and Lorraine's actually happen? Explain why or why not.

5. Contrast John and Lorraine's ability to rely on Dolly Racinski with their feeling that most adults, like their parents, offer little real support.

6. Compare and contrast John and Lorraine.

7. What is the significance of the dog Gus in the book? Would the book be just as effective without Gus' presence?

8. Discuss the way that humor appears in the book.

9. **The Pigman's Legacy** was first published in 1980. Are there aspects of the book that you think Paul Zindel would change if he were writing the book today? Be specific.

Extra Discussion Questions/Writing Assignments continued page 2

Critical/Personal Response

1. What faults in our society does Paul Zindel point out in **The Pigman's Legacy**?

2. Consider all of the references made to school and education in the book. What do you think is Paul Zindel's opinion of school?

3. Suppose this story were being told from Dolly Racinski's point of view. Do you think that the story would come across differently to students?

4. Do you think the relationship between John and Lorraine is realistic? Explain why or why not.

5. Do you think the relationship between Dolly and the Colonel is realistic? Explain why or why not.

6. How would the story have changed had the Colonel not died in the end?

7. If you were either John or Lorraine, would you have returned to the home of the old Pigman after you realized that a squatter was living there? Explain why or why not.

8. Paul Zindel includes some rather pointed comments about the medical profession in the book. What do you guess Zindel thinks of doctors and hospitals?

Personal Response

1. Did you enjoy reading **The Pigman's Legacy**? Explain why or why not.

2. What would you do if you found that someone like the Colonel was living in your neighborhood?

3. Why do you think students would tease someone like Dolly Racinski?

4. Do you believe that most parents are supportive of their children and willing and able to help them? Explain why or why not.

5. Do you think that someone in his or her sixties is old? Explain why or why not.

Lesson Fifteen

Objectives
1. To review ideas presented in the book
2. To show students specific quotations in the book that are important to theme, and/or character or plot development, and/or serve to involve the reader in the book

Activity #1
Distribute the Quotations Worksheet. Assign each student one quotation. Tell students that they are to think about their quotations and try to think of some reasons why their quotations would be significant to the theme or character or plot development or serve to involve the reader in the book. After giving students a few minutes to think, begin discussing each quotation, using the students' thoughts as a springboard.

Quotations Worksheet
The Pigman's Legacy

Note: Chapters are marked by the number of the chapter (1, 2, 3, etc.)

1. I never used to like reading either because a lot of my teachers made me read stuff I didn't need. (1)

2. As usual, I should never have let John write the first chapter. (2)

3. There was a face in the window. Dark, ominous eyes staring out into the street at me—and I knew they could see my eyes staring back. (2)

4. My mother, the Old Lady, is reading some book which has to do with her right to say "no" without feeling guilty whenever she gets an urge to run outside and lemon Pledge the sidewalk. (3)

5. And another thing, our Pigman was one guy who would do something like come back from the grave to let us know he was still thinking about us. (3)

6. If I had known then what was going to happen, I think I would have just cut out my tongue and gotten on a slow boat to China. (3)

7. And what happened next almost gave me a thrombosis. (3)

8. We watched in terror as the owner of the voice from the other side started to open the door. (3)

9. I think dead people work it that way. People die on you and then they send out vibes that give you another chance to make things better. (3)

10. Somehow when John touched me I felt again the kiss he had given me the night before—the kiss that reminded me of one of the most important things I've ever read in psychology, and that is that a person is what he does, not what he says. (6)

11. "The only game I know is the Game of Life," the old man finally wheezed, and his words riveted us because that was really the kind of game that the Pigman would know about. (6)

12. "I *am* telling the truth. Besides, this is no time to argue with your chauffeur. You know my father lets me drive the car." (7)

Quotations Worksheet continued page 2

13. We had come face to face with a giant plaque on the wall that was a full-color, three-dimensional, four-foot dinosaur. (7)

14. "I feel like I'm standing in a mausoleum," Lorraine said. "That's what this is." (7)

15. Gus barked, then jumped past me back into the car and started licking the Colonel's face. It took no more than a few seconds to revive the old man, and he woke up patting the dog on the head. (9)

16. "Haven't you got Medicare?" the mean nurse pursued. (9)

17. We're a family of untouchables, and if you think that sort of thing doesn't rub off on the kids, you're crazy. (9)

18. And even though she was only sixty years old, we knew from the other conversations with her that she was looking farther down the line and knew all about the way that United States government makes old people go broke. (10)

19. Sometimes I wish schools could just teach sex ignorance courses so I could spend more time being myself and less time worrying about what everybody else is doing. (10)

20. It was really great that the old guy wanted to lay a diamond on Dolly. The only thing shiny I ever saw my father buy for my mother was a soup pot. (11)

21. How could I tell them that I'd lost everything? How could I tell them? (11)

22. Then Dolly did something very strange. She moved us away from the Colonel's table and whispered to us. "It's all right. Don't worry about it."

23. "I want you to have this, Dolly. I want you to wear this and always think of me." (12)

24. Lorraine and I stood mute and helpless, and we were so grateful for having an adult help us for a change. (13)

25. Our legacy was *love*. (14)

Lesson Sixteen

Objective
To give students the opportunity to give updates on their projects (Project Aging) **or**
to encourage students in other ways to move beyond the parameters of **The Pigman's Legacy** to gain a better understanding of the concerns of older people in our society

Activity
Use this class period to have students give updates on their projects. If you decided against doing the whole project, this might be a good time to have students consider the ramifications of growing older in America. Let students brainstorm a list of potential concerns of older people. As each student suggests a concern, have that student write the concern on the black board. Then, when you have a list of things on the board, spend some time discussing possible ways that the concerns could be addressed.

Lesson Seventeen

Objectives
1. To give students an opportunity to report on their nonfiction reading assignments.
2. To broaden students' knowledge of the topics surrounding **The Pigman's Legacy**
3. To be sure that students are prepared for the Unit Test following this lesson

Activity #1
Ask each student to give a brief oral report about the nonfiction work he or she read for the nonfiction reading assignment. Your criteria for evaluating this report will vary depending on the level of your students. You may wish for students to give a complete report without using notes of any kind, or you may want students to read directly from a written report, or you may want to do something in between these two extremes. Just make sure that students understand your criteria in time to prepare their reports.

Start with one student's report. After that, ask if anyone else in the class has read on a topic related to the first student's report. If no one has, choose another student at random. After each report, be sure to ask if anyone has a report related to the one just completed. That will help keep a continuity during the discussion of the reports.

Activity #2
Remind students that the Unit Test will be given during the next class meeting. Stress the review of the Study Guides and their class notes as a last-minute, brush-up review.

Lesson Eighteen

Objective
To test the students' understanding of the main ideas and themes in **The Pigman's Legacy**.

Activity #1
Distribute the unit tests. Go over the instructions in detail and allow the students the entire class period to complete the exam.

Activity #2
Collect all test papers and assigned books prior to the end of the class period.

NOTES ABOUT THE UNIT TESTS IN THIS UNIT
Five different unit tests follow.

The **two short answer unit tests** are based primarily on facts from the novel and are followed by answer keys.

The **one advanced short answer unit test** is based on the extra discussion questions and quotations. Use the matching key for Short Answer Test #2 to check the correlating section of the advanced short answer test. There is no key for the short answer questions and quotations since these are relatively subjective and will be based on your class discussions.

There are **two multiple choice unit tests**. Following the two unit tests is an answer sheet on which students should mark their answers. The same answer sheet should be used for both tests. Following the student' answer sheet for the multiple choice tests are two keys: one for Multiple Choice Test #1 and one for Multiple Choice Test #2.

The short answer tests have a vocabulary section. Choose ten of the vocabulary words from this unit, read them orally, and have the students write them down. Then, either have students write a definition or use the words in sentences.

Use these words for the vocabulary section of the advanced short answer test:

foibles	undulating	indigent
mortified	surreptitiously	vivaciousness
serendipity	pubescent	apparition
geology	abstinence	ecstasy
platonically	gruff	mute

UNIT TESTS

Short Answer Unit Test #1 - Pigman's Legacy

I. Matching/Identify

____ 1. Mrs. Jensen   A. the original Pigman

____ 2. Dolly Racinski   B. the Colonel's dog

____ 3. Gus   C. cafeteria sweeper who marries the Colonel

____ 4. Mr. Pignati   D. one of the two kids in the story

____ 5. John Conlan   E. the Colonel

____ 6. Parker Glenville   F. John's father

____ 7. Lorraine   G. Lorraine's mother

____ 8. Bore   H. one of the two kids in the story

II. Short Answer

1. What gift do mean people say John and Lorraine gave the original Pigman?

2. What kind of help did John and Lorraine expect to get from the adult world?

3. Why does Lorraine think Mr. Pignati has come back from the dead?

4. What present did John and Lorraine take to the old man when they returned?

5. What does the old man say is the only game he knows?

Short Answer Unit Test #1 continued page 2

6. What is the wall the old man says is blocking John's way on the road?

7. What were on the three large plaques that were in the town house?

8. Why was the Colonel in trouble with the IRS?

9. What present did the Colonel give to Dolly as they returned home from Atlantic City?

10. What was the legacy of John and Lorraine's Pigman?

III. Essay

What are the three most important lessons about life that a reader can learn from reading **The Pigman's Legacy**? Be sure to write a complete essay, including introduction and conclusion. And be sure to use specific examples from the book.

Short Answer Unit Test #1 continued page 3

IV. Vocabulary

Listen to the vocabulary word and spell it. After you have spelled all the words, go back and write down the definitions.

1.

2.

3.

4.

5.

6.

7.

8.

9.

10.

Key: Short Answer Unit Test #1 - Pigman's Legacy

I.   Matching/Identify

G	1. Mrs. Jensen	A.	the original Pigman
C	2. Dolly Racinski	B.	the Colonel's dog
B	3. Gus	C.	cafeteria sweeper who marries the Colonel
A	4. Mr. Pignati	D.	one of the two kids in the story
D or H	5. John Conlan	E.	the Colonel
E	6. Parker Glenville	F.	John's father
D or H	7. Lorraine	G.	Lorraine's mother
F	8. Bore	H.	one of the two kids in the story

II.   Short Answer

1. What gift do mean people say John and Lorraine gave the original Pigman?
   They say that John and Lorraine gave the Pigman "death."

2. What kind of help did John and Lorraine expect to get from the adult world?
   They expected no help at all.

3. Why does Lorraine think Mr. Pignati has come back from the dead?
   She thinks he has come back to give her and John a message.

4. What present did John and Lorraine take to the old man when they returned?
   They took him some marble pecan fudge.

5. What does the old man say is the only game he knows?
   He says the only game he knows is The Game of Life.

6. What is the wall the old man says is blocking John's way on the road?
   The old man says the wall of death is blocking John's way.

Key: Short Answer Unit Test #1 continued page 2

7. What were on the three large plaques that were in the town house?
   There were dinosaurs on the plaques.

8. Why was the Colonel in trouble with the IRS?
   He had not paid his taxes for many years.

9. What present did the Colonel give to Dolly as they returned home from Atlantic City?
   He gave her his special medallion.

10. What was the legacy of John and Lorraine's Pigman?
    The legacy of the Pigman was love.

III. Essay
What are the three most important lessons about life that a reader can learn from reading **The Pigman's Legacy**? Be sure to write a complete essay, including introduction and conclusion. And be sure to use specific examples from the book.

IV. Vocabulary
Choose ten of the vocabulary words to read orally for the vocabulary section of this unit test.

Short Answer Unit Test #2 - Pigman's Legacy

I. Matching/Identify

____ 1. Lorraine   A. the original Pigman

____ 2. Parker Glenville   B. the Colonel's dog

____ 3. Bore   C. cafeteria sweeper who marries the Colonel

____ 4. Gus   D. one of the two kids in the story

____ 5. Mrs. Jensen   E. the Colonel

____ 6. John Conlan   F. John's father

____ 7. Dolly Racinski   G. Lorraine's mother

____ 8. Mr. Pignati   H. one of the two kids in the story

II. Short Answer

1. What does the Pigman kill, according to Lorraine?

2. What terms does John use for his mother and father?

3. Why does Dolly especially like John and Lorraine?

4. A part of what animal was on the old man's medallion?

5. What has John's driving experience been prior to driving the old man's car?

Short Answer Unit Test #2 continued page 2

6. How did the German shepherd wake up the Colonel?

7. What did the Colonel sell to raise money to go to Atlantic City?

8. What did John ultimately do with the money the Colonel and Dolly won?

9. After she got over her initial shock, how did Dolly respond to losing the money?

10. What does John say to Lorraine at the end of the book?

III. Essay
One of the main issues in **The Pigman's Legacy** is what it is like to be a teenager. What do you think is Paul Zindel's view of teenagers (adolescents) and their situation now that you have read his book? Be sure to write a good introduction and conclusion and to give specific examples from the book.

Short Answer Unit Test #2 continued page 3

IV. Vocabulary

Listen to the vocabulary word and spell it. After you have spelled all the words, go back and write down the definitions.

1.

2.

3.

4.

5.

6.

7.

8.

9.

10.

Key: Short Answer Unit Test #2 - Pigman's Legacy

I. Matching/Identify

DorH 1. Lorraine   A. the original Pigman

E   2. Parker Glenville   B. the Colonel's dog

F   3. Bore   C. cafeteria sweeper who marries the Colonel

B   4. Gus   D. one of the two kids in the story

G   5. Mrs. Jensen   E. the Colonel

DorH 6. John Conlan   F. John's father

C   7. Dolly Racinski   G. Lorraine's mother

A   8. Mr. Pignati   H. one of the two kids in the story

II. Short Answer

1. What does the Pigman kill, according to Lorraine?
   The Pigman kills a person's childhood.

2. What terms does John use for his mother and father?
   John refers to his mother as the Old Lady and to his father as Bore.

3. Why does Dolly especially like John and Lorraine?
   She especially likes them because they are kind to her.

4. What kind of animal horn was on the old man's medallion?
   It is the horn of a rhino.

5. What has John's driving experience been prior to driving the old man's car?
   His only experience has been backing his father's car out of the driveway.

6. How did the German shepherd wake up the Colonel?
   He woke the Colonel up by licking his face.

7. What did the Colonel sell to raise money to go to Atlantic City?
   He sold his collection of silver dollars.

Key: Short Answer Unit Test #2 continued page 2

8. What did John ultimately do with the money the Colonel and Dolly won?
   John lost the money gambling.

9. After she got over her initial shock, how did Dolly respond to losing the money?
   Dolly said that it was all right and John shouldn't worry about it.

10. What does John say to Lorraine at the end of the book?
    He says, "I want to spend the rest of my life with you."

III. Essay
   One of the main issues in **The Pigman's Legacy** is what it is like to be a teenager. What do you think is Paul Zindel's view of teenagers (adolescents) and their situation now that you have read his book? Be sure to write a good introduction and conclusion and to give specific examples from the book.

IV. Vocabulary
   Choose ten of the vocabulary words to read orally for the vocabulary section of the test.

Advanced Short Answer Unit Test - Pigman's Legacy

I. Matching/Identify

____ 1. Lorraine   A. the original Pigman

____ 2. Parker Glenville B. the Colonel's dog

____ 3. Bore   C. cafeteria sweeper who marries the Colonel

____ 4. Gus   D. one of the two kids in the story

____ 5. Mrs. Jensen   E. the Colonel

____ 6. John Conlan   F. John's father

____ 7. Dolly Racinski   G. Lorraine's mother

____ 8. Mr. Pignati   H. one of the two kids in the story

II. Short Answer

1. Compare and contrast the Colonel and Dolly Racinski.

2. Are the characters in **The Pigman's Legacy** believable or not? Explain why or why not.

3. Is the plot of **The Pigman's Legacy** realistic? Could a story like John and Lorraine's actually happen? Explain why or why not.

4. Compare and contrast John and Lorraine.

Advanced Short Answer Unit Test continued page 2

5. What is the significance of the dog Gus in the book? Would the book be just as effective without Gus' presence?

III. Essay

Choose one of the characters in **The Pigman's Legacy** and tell, in a fully developed essay, in what way(s) that character develops in the book. Be sure that you can show that the person is different at or near the end of the book than he or she was at the beginning. Use specific details from the book to support your point of view.

Advanced Short Answer Unit Test continued page 3

IV. Vocabulary

Define each of the vocabulary words below. After you have defined them all, write a paragraph in which you use all the words. The paragraph must in some way related to **The Pigman's Legacy**.

1. condone
2. sublimation
3. dossier
4. reverie
5. undulating
6. stupor
7. surreptitiously
8. surveillance
9. serendipity
10. mausoleum

Paragraph using all words

Multiple Choice-Matching Unit Test #1 - Pigman's Legacy

I. Matching/Identify

____ 1. Mrs. Jensen   A. the original Pigman

____ 2. Dolly Racinski   B. the Colonel's dog

____ 3. Gus   C. cafeteria sweeper who marries the Colonel

____ 4. Mr. Pignati   D. one of the two kids in the story

____ 5. John Conlan   E. the Colonel

____ 6. Parker Glenville   F. John's father

____ 7. Lorraine   G. Lorraine's mother

____ 8. Bore   H. one of the two kids in the story

II. Short Answer

1. What gift do mean people say John and Lorraine gave the original Pigman?
    a. "Death"
    b. Lots of happiness
    c. A new car
    d. The keys to an apartment

2, What kind of help did John and Lorraine expect to get from the adult world?
    a. Only expert, caring help
    b. No help at all
    c. Some help if they asked for it carefully
    d. Some help if they hadn't done anything illegal

3. Why does Lorraine think Mr. Pignati has come back from the dead?
    a. To give her and John a message
    b. To get revenge on his enemies
    c. To teach them a lesson about practical jokes
    d. To find out why he died in the first place

Multiple Choice-Matching Unit Test #1 continued page 2

4. What present did John and Lorraine take to the old man when they returned?
   a. A bagel
   b. A bag of groceries
   c. Some marble pecan fudge
   d. A pack of cigarettes

5. What does the old man say is the only game he knows?
   a. Chess
   b. Mahjong
   c. The Game of Life
   d. Football

6. What is the wall the old man says is blocking John's way on the road?
   a. The wall of death
   b. John's lack of sexual experience
   c. John's inhibitions
   d. Thoughts of girls

7. What were on the three large plaques that were in the town house?
   a. Pictures of old war heroes
   b. Dinosaurs
   c. Pictures of British royalty
   d. Congratulatory notes to the Colonel

8. Why was the Colonel in trouble with the IRS?
   a. Because he forgot to pay his taxes the year before
   b. Because he had not paid his real estate taxes for many years
   c. Because he lied about his income
   d. Because he lied about charitable deductions

9. What present did the Colonel give to Dolly as they returned home from Atlantic City?
   a. A silver dollar
   b. His special medallion
   c. A huge diamond ring
   d. A pair of diamond earrings

10. What was the legacy of John and Lorraine's Pigman?
    a. Love
    b. Wariness
    c. Adolescent fixations
    d. Death

Multiple Choice-Matching Unit Test #1 continued page 3

III. Essay
   If you were going to recommend **The Pigman's Legacy** to a student two or three years younger than you are, what would you say the book would teach him or her? Write an essay explaining your answer. Be sure to give specific examples from the book.

Multiple Choice-Matching Unit Test #1 continued page 4

IV. Vocabulary   Match the words and definitions.

1. memorial   A. site revered for its associations
2. fleecing   B. a state of abstract musing
3. medallion   C. ability to make fortunate discoveries by accident
4. mausoleum   D. said
5. surreptitiously   E. hypnotized
6. serendipity   F. deliberate restraining of oneself; not indulging
7. Keogh   G. carved or etched into a surface
8. shrine   H. dummies
9. blurted   I. a large medal
10. reverie   J. defrauding of money or property; swindling
11. reincarnated   K. commemorative, serving as a reminder of
12. mannequins   L. reborn
13. mesmerized   M. impoverished; needy
14. abstinence   N. brief and unfriendly; harsh
15. anguish   O. a large stately tomb
16. engraved   P. secretly
17. indigent   Q. retirement plan for the self-employed
18. dossier   R. agonizing physical or mental pain
19. omen   S. collection of papers about a particular person
20. gruff   T. sign of future good or evil

Multiple Choice-Matching Unit Test #2 - Pigman's Legacy

I. Matching/Identify

____ 1. Lorraine   A. the original Pigman

____ 2. Parker Glenville   B. the Colonel's dog

____ 3. Bore   C. cafeteria sweeper who marries the Colonel

____ 4. Gus   D. one of the two kids in the story

____ 5. Mrs. Jensen   E. the Colonel

____ 6. John Conlan   F. John's father

____ 7. Dolly Racinski   G. Lorraine's mother

____ 8. Mr. Pignati   H.. one of the two kids in the story

II. Short Answer
1. What does the Pigman kill, according to Lorraine?
   a. John and Lorraine's pet rabbit
   b. A person's childhood
   c. His next door neighbor
   d. His wife

2. What terms does John use for his mother and father?
   a. Ma and Pa
   b. The Old Lady and Bore
   c. Carol and Jim
   d. Mama and Papa

3. Why does Dolly especially like John and Lorraine?
   a. Because they are kind to her
   b. Because they like her special earrings
   c. Because they call her Mrs. Racinski
   d. Because they bring her gifts every Friday

Multiple Choice-Matching Unit Test #2 continued page 2

4. A part of what animal was on the old man's medallion?
   a. A horse
   b. A dog
   c. A cat
   d. A rhino

5. What has John's driving experience been prior to driving the old man's car?
   a. He once drove into New York City.
   b. He has backed his father's car out of the driveway.
   c. He has driven but only with a veteran driver in the car with him.
   d. He has driven only about 100 miles around town.

6. How did the German shepherd wake up the Colonel?
   a. He barked really loudly.
   b. He howled.
   c. He licked the Colonel's face.
   d. He whined for a long time.

7. What did the Colonel sell to raise money to go to Atlantic City?
   a. His special necklace
   b. Some magic beans
   c. A special token given to him by the King of Sweden
   d. His collection of silver dollars.

8. What did John ultimately do with the money that the Colonel and Dolly won?
   a. He doubled the money at the blackjack table.
   b. He deposited it in a local bank.
   c. He shared it with Lorraine.
   d. He lost the money gambling.

9. After she got over her initial shock, how did Dolly respond to losing the money?
   a. She called the police.
   b. She slapped John.
   c. She said that it was all right and John shouldn't worry about it.
   d. She blamed Lorraine.

10. What does John say to Lorraine at the end of the book?
    a. "I don't think you handled yourself very well today."
    b. "I really had a swell time today."
    c. "Let's do it all over again tomorrow, Lorraine."
    d. "I want to spend my life with you."

III. Essay

One of the main issues in **The Pigman's Legacy** is what it is like to be an older American. What do you think is Paul Zindel's view of older people and their situation now that you have read his book? Be sure to write a good introduction and conclusion and to give specific examples from the book.

IV. Vocabulary   Match the vocabulary words and definitions.

1. memorial   A. sign of future good or evil
2. fleecing   B. a state of abstract musing
3. medallion   C. ability to make fortunate discoveries by accident
4. mausoleum   D. reborn
5. surreptitiously E. collection of papers about a particular person
6. serendipity   F. deliberate restraining of oneself; not indulging
7. Keogh   G. carved or etched into a surface
8. shrine   H. site revered for its associations
9. blurted   I. secretly
10. reverie   J. defrauding of money or property; swindling
11. reincarnated   K. commemorative, serving as a reminder of
12. mannequins   L. said
13. mesmerized   M. impoverished; needy
14. abstinence   N. brief and unfriendly; harsh
15. anguish   O. a large stately tomb
16. engraved   P. a large medal
17. indigent   Q. retirement plan for the self-employed
18. dossier   R. agonizing physical or mental pain
19. omen   S. hypnotized
20. gruff   T. dummies

ANSWER SHEET - *Pigman's Legacy*
Multiple Choice Unit Test

I. Matching

1. ____
2. ____
3. ____
4. ____
5. ____
6. ____
7. ____
8. ____

II. Multiple Choice

1. (A) (B) (C) (D)
2. (A) (B) (C) (D)
3. (A) (B) (C) (D)
4. (A) (B) (C) (D)
5. (A) (B) (C) (D)
6. (A) (B) (C) (D)
7. (A) (B) (C) (D)
8. (A) (B) (C) (D)
9. (A) (B) (C) (D)
10. (A) (B) (C) (D)

III. Vocabulary

1. ____
2. ____
3. ____
4. ____
5. ____
6. ____
7. ____
8. ____
9. ____
10. ____
11. ____
12. ____
13. ____
14. ____
15. ____
16. ____
17. ____
18. ____
19. ____
20. ____

ANSWER SHEET KEY - *Pigman's Legacy*
Multiple Choice Unit Test 1

I. Matching
1.   G
2.   C
3.   B
4.   A
5.   DorH
6.   E
7.   DorH
8.   F

II. Multiple Choice

1. ( ) (B) (C) (D)
2. (A) ( ) (C) (D)
3. ( ) (B) (C) (D)
4. (A) (B) ( ) (D)
5. (A) (B) ( ) (D)
6. ( ) (B) (C) (D)
7. (A) ( ) (C) (D)
8. (A) ( ) (C) (D)
9. (A) ( ) (C) (D)
10. ( ) (B) (C) (D)

III. Vocabulary
1.   K
2.   J
3.   I
4.   O
5.   P
6.   C
7.   Q
8.   A
9.   D
10.   B
11.   L
12.   H
13.   E
14.   F
15.   R
16.   G
17.   M
18.   S
19.   T
20.   N

ANSWER SHEET KEY - *Pigman's Legacy*
Multiple Choice Unit Test 2

I. Matching

1. __DorH__
2. __E__
3. __F__
4. __B__
5. __G__
6. __DorH__
7. __C__
8. __A__

II. Multiple Choice

1. (A) ( ) (C) (D)
2. (A) ( ) (C) (D)
3. ( ) (B) (C) (D)
4. (A) (B) (C) ( )
5. (A) ( ) (C) (D)
6. (A) (B) ( ) (D)
7. (A) (B) (C) ( )
8. (A) (B) (C) ( )
9. (A) (B) ( ) (D)
10. (A) (B) (C) ( )

III. Vocabulary

1. __K__
2. __J__
3. __P__
4. __O__
5. __I__
6. __C__
7. __Q__
8. __H__
9. __L__
10. __B__
11. __D__
12. __T__
13. __S__
14. __F__
15. __R__
16. __G__
17. __M__
18. __E__
19. __A__
20. __N__

UNIT RESOURCE MATERIALS

Bulletin Board Ideas - The Pigman's Legacy

1. Have each student in the class choose his or her favorite quotation from the book. Then ask each student to write his or her quote very clearly and carefully on a colored index card and to explain briefly on the card why they think the quote is interesting. Post all of the index cards on the bulletin board. If your class is large and your bulletin board small, consider rotating the cards.

2. There is a lot of information available about Paul Zindel, the author of **The Pigman's Legacy**. Have students research him and his work   Then have each student choose one thing about Paul Zindel that he or she finds interesting. Put some brightly colored paper on the bulletin board and have students write in their most interesting piece of information about Paul Zindel. Be prepared yourself with some information and perhaps the names of his other books so that the information about him will be complete.

3. Pretend that the bulletin board in the classroom is a spot in a busy city where people write lots of graffiti. Invite students to take a minute at the beginning or end of each class period to write something that expresses their own personal feelings about the book, its ideas, its character, or its author. Set some guidelines about appropriateness of comments and then let students write whatever they want.

4. Save a portion of a black board to use as a bulletin board for rotating comments. Start each day with a comment that might be made by one of the four characters in **The Pigman's Legacy**. Sign your comment with the name of one of the characters. Invite students to make comments about the one you put up and sign their comment with the name of one of the other three characters. Try to build up some suspense every day about what comment will appear from which character. None of the comments need be from the book, only in character for the person making it.

5. Make a bulletin board listing the vocabulary words for this unit. As you complete sections of the book and discuss the vocabulary for each section, write the definitions on the bulletin board. Encourage students to look at the board often so that they learn the words easily.

6. With the permission of the student writers, post the best writing assignments done for this unit.

7. If you have students who can draw, ask them to sketch a picture of one of the major characters or a scene from **The Pigman's Legacy** and post it on the bulletin board.

8. Ask students to look through magazines and find pictures of people that look like their idea of each of the four characters in **The Pigman's Legacy**. Get the students to post their pictures on the bulletin board labeled with the names of the characters the pictures make them think of. If you run short of material to cover one day, you could point to each picture on the bulletin board and see if there is consensus in the class about whether the pictures are like the characters or not. Even if the class disagrees with a particular association, that doesn't make the picture chosen wrong. It only means that a student has his or her own conception of what the character is like. Maybe that student will feel free to explain what he or she is thinking about the character. This might enlarge everyone's thoughts about the characters and the book.

Extra Activities - The Pigman's Legacy

One of the difficulties in teaching a book is that not all students read at the same speed. One student who likes to read may take the book home and finish it in a day or two. Sometimes a few students finish the in-class assignments early. The problem, then, is finding suitable extra activities for students.

One useful thing to do is to keep a little library in the classroom. For this unit on **The Pigman's Legacy**, you might check out from the school or local library other related books and articles about student/parent relationships, psychology, marriage, death, zoos and animals, pigs, hobbies, etc. If possible, also have on hand some copies of Paul Zindel's other books so that students can read something else by the author if they choose to do so.

Other things you may keep on hand are puzzles. There are some in this unit directly relating to **The Pigman's Legacy**. Feel free to duplicate them for your students' use.

Some students may like to draw or paint. You might devise a contest or allow some extra-credit grade for students who draw characters or scenes from **The Pigman's Legacy**. Note, too, that if the students do not want to keep their drawings, you may pick up some extra bulletin board materials this way. If you have a contest and you supply the prize (a CD, a copy of another book by Zindel, a copy of a book on a subject similar to that in **The Pigman's Legacy**, for example), you could possibly make the drawing itself a non-refundable entry fee. Make sure you assure students that you will continue to place their name on the board with the drawing. This can assure a student that years into the future his or her drawing will still be in his or her old classroom.

The pages which follow contain games, puzzles, and worksheets. The keys, when appropriate, immediately follow the puzzle or worksheet. There are two main groups of activities: one group for the unit: that is, generally relating to the text of The Pigman's Legacy and another group of activities related strictly to the vocabulary words in The Pigman's Legacy.

Directions for these games, puzzles, and worksheets are self-explanatory. The object here is to provide you with extra materials you may use in any way you choose.

More Activities - The Pigman's Legacy

1. Have students choose to "be" either John Conlan or Lorraine Jensen. Ask them to keep a journal daily in which they write about what happens to them—but in the voice and character of one of the teenage characters. Everything they write, even if they want to make comments about class to you, should be done in character.

2. Encourage students to write to a local retirement community and get the names of a few of the residents there. Then have students establish pen-pal relationships with the residents in the community. If things work out well, the students may well get return communications from the residents.

3. Encourage students to write one of the scenes in the book from the standpoint of Gus, the Colonel's dog. This kind of exercise will make students look at the details of the book differently than they did on a first reading.

4. Have students pretend to be either John or Lorraine and ask them to write letters to their parents. In the letters they should try to explain how the parents' views and actions are creating distance between them and their children.

5. Let interested students "teach" a class one day. If the number of interested students is sufficient, you could allow the students to work together, make a clear plan, and actually teach a whole class. Feel free to share your daily lesson plans with the students as they prepare to teach.

6. Have students design a CD cover for a piece of music that they think John and Lorraine might like to make together. They should name the piece of music and then design the cover in whatever way they think is appropriate.

7. Ask students each to write an obituary for the Colonel. They could use as models one of the obituaries appearing in your local newspaper or a paper like *The New York Times*.

8. Make a bulletin board with telephone numbers students can call for advice in case they want additional information about the subjects presented in **The Pigman's Legacy**. For instance, if students wanted information about retirement communities, abuse of old people, Medicare, retirement plans, or whatever, they would be able to gain easy access to them. Students might want this information for purposes of class or for real life situations concerning their grandparents or older friends, neighbors, and relatives.

WORD SEARCH - PIGMAN'S LEGACY

Words are placed backwards, forward, diagonally, up and down. Words listed below are included in the maze. Circle the hidden vocabulary words in the maze.

```
I R S P R I E S T S W E D E N G X D K X
H D E O R T C Y S Z J F L T J U K X E F
X L R L E A N Q U Y T R K S Y S D P O C
S Z E T L N E F R X J U L D H N X M G D
V F N E L G C B U P R O M I S E R J H K
J H D R I I S K A D S F K K F E J H C L
W H I G V P E U S W G Y Y E K E W L A G
Q J P E N A L N O C J E C A S L E D N Y
C S I I E W O M G B N D B H E R S O I S
B F T S L F D H E O V E N D O R M L P F
T A Y T G C A L T N D S N B L L C L S G
C U R S E S S S U K I N Z T B O Y W N
P W K F H K E Z T C Z Y K K M Y X G T S
G E R M A N H S S Y D H Y O K X G N Y T
P Q N O I L L A D E M M T T H Z F T B V
C J B H Y E L L O W C H I L D H O O D K
A I R E T E F A C D L X R Z Z Y F J G Y
A T L A N T I C B M R K G S M K W B N L
```

ADOLESCENCE	DOLLY	KEOGH	PROMISE	TOMB
ATLANTIC	FOUR	KIDS	PSYCHOLOGY	YELLOW
BARF	FUDGE	LIFE	RHINESTONE	ZINDEL
BORE	GERMAN	MEDALLION	SERENDIPITY	
CAFETERIA	GLENVILLE	PAUL	SPINACH	
CHILDHOOD	GUS	PIGNATI	STEGOSAURUS	
CONLAN	IRS	POLTERGEIST	STUDEBAKER	
CURSES	JOKES	PRIEST	SWEDEN	

ANSWER KEY - PIGMAN'S LEGACY

```
I R S P R I E S T S W E D E N G       K
    E O   T C   S             U       E
    R L E A N   U     R   S   S       O
    E T L N E F R   J U L D           G
    N E L G C   U P R O M I S E R     H
    D R I I S   A D S F K K F E       C
    I G V P E U S   G Y   E K E       A
    P E N A L N O C   E C A S L E D   N
    I I E   O G   N   B H E R     O   I
B   T S L   D   E O   E   D O     L   P
  A Y T G   A   T   D   N B       L   S
C U R S E S   S S U   I       B O Y
      F     E   T   Z         M   G
G E R M A N   S               O       Y
    N O I L L A D E M   T
      H Y E L L O W C H I L D H O O D
A I R E T E F A C
A T L A N T I C
```

Pigman's Legacy Crossword

Across

3. First name of author
5. Lorraine reads a lot of books about ____.
10. Dolly wore what kind of earrings?
12. What was the Colonel wearing around his neck?
13. Phony name originally give by the Colonel
14. Who did the Colonel ask to see before he died?
18. Author's last name
19. The Colonel was knighted by the King of ____.
20. A mausoleum is a large, stately ____.
21. The Colonel wanted to go to ____ City.
23. How does John refer to his father?
24. Gift that John and Lorraine took to the Colonel
25. How John and Lorraine refer to themselves
26. A retirement plan for the self-employed.
27. Name of the introduction to the book, The ____

Down

1. Dolly and the Colonel won ____ Thousand Dollars.
2. John no longer plays many practical ____.
3. A mischievous ghost
4. The only game the Colonel knows is The Game of ____.
6. John's last name
7. Color of the Colonel's car
8. Word John uses to be 'throw up'
9. Ms. Racinski's first name
11. What government agency does the Colonel fear most?
13. Colonel's real last name
15. Dinosaur with bony plates on its back
16. Last name of the original Pigman
17. Gus is a ____ shepard.
19. Kind of car owned by the Colonel
22. What do @#$% and #@#$% represent in John's writing?

Pigman's Legacy Crossword Answer Key

							1 F			2 J		3 P	A	U	4 L
		5 P	S	Y	6 C	H	O	L	O	G	Y	O		O		I
					O		U			K		L			F
	7 Y		8 B		9 N		10 R	11 H	I	N	E	S	T	O	N	E
12 M	E	D	A	L	L	I	O	N		R		S		E	
	L		R		A		L		13 G	U	S		14 P	R	I	15 S	T
	L		F		N		L		L		16 P		G		T
	O			17 G			Y		E		18 Z	I	N	D	E	L	E
19 S	W	E	D	E	N				N		G		I		G
T				R					V		N		S		O
U		20 T	O	M	B				I		A		T		S
D				A			21 A	T	L	A	N	T	I	22 C		A
E				N					L				I		U
23 B	O	R	E		24 F	U	D	G	E				R		U
A										25 K	I	D	S		U
26 K	E	O	G	H									E		S
E							27 P	R	O	M	I	S	E	
R														

Across

3. First name of author
5. Lorraine reads a lot of books about ____.
10. Dolly wore what kind of earrings?
12. What was the Colonel wearing around his neck?
13. Phony name originally give by the Colonel
14. Who did the Colonel ask to see before he died?
18. Author's last name
19. The Colonel was knighted by the King of ____.
20. A mausoleum is a large, stately ____.
21. The Colonel wanted to go to ____ City.
23. How does John refer to his father?
24. Gift that John and Lorraine took to the Colonel
25. How John and Lorraine refer to themselves
26. A retirement plan for the self-employed.
27. Name of the introduction to the book, The ____

Down

1. Dolly and the Colonel won ____ Thousand Dollars.
2. John no longer plays many practical ____.
3. A mischievous ghost
4. The only game the Colonel knows is The Game of ____.
6. John's last name
7. Color of the Colonel's car
8. Word John uses to be 'throw up'
9. Ms. Racinski's first name
11. What government agency does the Colonel fear most?
13. Colonel's real last name
15. Dinosaur with bony plates on its back
16. Last name of the original Pigman
17. Gus is a ____ shepard.
19. Kind of car owned by the Colonel
22. What do @#$% and #@#$% represent in John's writing?

MATCHING QUIZ/ WORKSHEET 1 - The Pigman's Legacy

___ 1. POLTERGEIST   A. Colonel's real last name
___ 2. IRS   B. Word John uses to be 'throw up'
___ 3. ZINDEL   C. The Colonel wanted to go to ____ City.
___ 4. YELLOW   D. How John and Lorraine refer to themselves
___ 5. PRIEST   E. Last name of the original Pigman
___ 6. STEGOSAURUS   F. Faculty of making fortunate discoveries by accident
___ 7. DOLLY   G. Name of the introduction to the book, The ____
___ 8. CHILDHOOD   H. John no longer plays many practical ____.
___ 9. CAFETERIA   I. What do @#$% and #@#$% represent in John's writing?
___10. PIGNATI   J. A mischievous ghost
___11. GLENVILLE   K. Author's last name
___12. KEOGH   L. John's last name
___13. FOUR   M. Color of the Colonel's car
___14. KIDS   N. Who did the Colonel ask to see before he died?
___15. BARF   O. Dinosaur with bony plates on its back
___16. SERENDIPITY   P. What government agency does the Colonel fear most?
___17. CURSES   Q. Dolly and the Colonel won ____ Thousand Dollars.
___18. PSYCHOLOGY   R. Dolly works in the school ____.
___19. GUS   S. Period from puberty to maturity
___20. CONLAN   T. Ms. Racinski's first name
___21. RHINESTONE   U. A retirement plan for the self-employed.
___22. JOKES   V. Dolly wore what kind of earrings?
___23. ATLANTIC   W. Lorraine reads a lot of books about ____.
___24. PROMISE   X. A Pigman basically kills a kid's ____.
___25. ADOLESCENCE   Y. Phony name originally give by the Colonel

KEY: MATCHING QUIZ/ WORKSHEET 1 - The Pigman's Legacy

J - 1.	POLTERGEIST	A. Colonel's real last name
P - 2.	IRS	B. Word John uses to be 'throw up'
K - 3.	ZINDEL	C. The Colonel wanted to go to ____ City.
M - 4.	YELLOW	D. How John and Lorraine refer to themselves
N - 5.	PRIEST	E. Last name of the original Pigman
O - 6.	STEGOSAURUS	F. Faculty of making fortunate discoveries by accident
T - 7.	DOLLY	G. Name of the introduction to the book, The ____
X - 8.	CHILDHOOD	H. John no longer plays many practical ____.
R - 9.	CAFETERIA	I. What do @#$% and #@#$% represent in John's writing?
E -10.	PIGNATI	J. A mischievous ghost
A -11.	GLENVILLE	K. Author's last name
U -12.	KEOGH	L. John's last name
Q -13.	FOUR	M. Color of the Colonel's car
D -14.	KIDS	N. Who did the Colonel ask to see before he died?
B -15.	BARF	O. Dinosaur with bony plates on its back
F -16.	SERENDIPITY	P. What government agency does the Colonel fear most?
I -17.	CURSES	Q. Dolly and the Colonel won ____ Thousand Dollars.
W 18.	PSYCHOLOGY	R. Dolly works in the school ____.
Y -19.	GUS	S. Period from puberty to maturity
L -20.	CONLAN	T. Ms. Racinski's first name
V -21.	RHINESTONE	U. A retirement plan for the self-employed.
H -22.	JOKES	V. Dolly wore what kind of earrings?
C -23.	ATLANTIC	W. Lorraine reads a lot of books about ____.
G -24.	PROMISE	X. A Pigman basically kills a kid's ____.
S -25.	ADOLESCENCE	Y. Phony name originally give by the Colonel

MATCHING QUIZ/ WORKSHEET 2 - The Pigman's Legacy

___ 1. JOKES   A. How does John refer to his father?
___ 2. IRS   B. Dolly works in the school ____.
___ 3. PIGNATI   C. What do @#$% and #@#$% represent in John's writing?
___ 4. GUS   D. A Pigman basically kills a kid's ____.
___ 5. KIDS   E. Ms. Racinski's first name
___ 6. CAFETERIA   F. The Colonel was knighted by the King of ____.
___ 7. DOLLY   G. Gift that John and Lorraine took to the Colonel
___ 8. FUDGE   H. Kind of cigarettes Lorraine wants John to smoke
___ 9. YELLOW   I. What government agency does the Colonel fear most?
___10. POLTERGEIST   J. Lorraine reads a lot of books about ____.
___11. SERENDIPITY   K. John no longer plays many practical ____.
___12. FOUR   L. Last name of the original Pigman
___13. GLENVILLE   M. Word John uses to be 'throw up'
___14. BARF   N. How John and Lorraine refer to themselves
___15. PRIEST   O. Name of the introduction to the book, The ____
___16. PROMISE   P. Who did the Colonel ask to see before he died?
___17. SWEDEN   Q. Phony name originally give by the Colonel
___18. CURSES   R. Faculty of making fortunate discoveries by accident
___19. CONLAN   S. John's last name
___20. BORE   T. A mischievous ghost
___21. STEGOSAURUS   U. Colonel's real last name
___22. CHILDHOOD   V. Color of the Colonel's car
___23. PSYCHOLOGY   W. What was the Colonel wearing around his neck?
___24. SPINACH   X. Dinosaur with bony plates on its back
___25. MEDALLION   Y. Dolly and the Colonel won ____ Thousand Dollars.

KEY: MATCHING QUIZ/ WORKSHEET 2 - The Pigman's Legacy

K - 1.	JOKES	A. How does John refer to his father?
I - 2.	IRS	B. Dolly works in the school ____.
L - 3.	PIGNATI	C. What do @#$% and #@$% represent in John's writing?
Q - 4.	GUS	D. A Pigman basically kills a kid's ____.
N - 5.	KIDS	E. Ms. Racinski's first name
B - 6.	CAFETERIA	F. The Colonel was knighted by the King of ____.
E - 7.	DOLLY	G. Gift that John and Lorraine took to the Colonel
G - 8.	FUDGE	H. Kind of cigarettes Lorraine wants John to smoke
V - 9.	YELLOW	I. What government agency does the Colonel fear most?
T - 10.	POLTERGEIST	J. Lorraine reads a lot of books about ____.
R - 11.	SERENDIPITY	K. John no longer plays many practical ____.
Y - 12.	FOUR	L. Last name of the original Pigman
U - 13.	GLENVILLE	M. Word John uses to be 'throw up'
M - 14.	BARF	N. How John and Lorraine refer to themselves
P - 15.	PRIEST	O. Name of the introduction to the book, The ____
O - 16.	PROMISE	P. Who did the Colonel ask to see before he died?
F - 17.	SWEDEN	Q. Phony name originally give by the Colonel
C - 18.	CURSES	R. Faculty of making fortunate discoveries by accident
S - 19.	CONLAN	S. John's last name
A - 20.	BORE	T. A mischievous ghost
X - 21.	STEGOSAURUS	U. Colonel's real last name
D - 22.	CHILDHOOD	V. Color of the Colonel's car
J - 23.	PSYCHOLOGY	W. What was the Colonel wearing around his neck?
H - 24.	SPINACH	X. Dinosaur with bony plates on its back
W 25.	MEDALLION	Y. Dolly and the Colonel won ____ Thousand Dollars.

JUGGLE LETTER REVIEW GAME - PIGMAN'S LEGACY

SKID	KIDS	How John and Lorraine refer to themselves
LEDNIZ	ZINDEL	Author's last name
INTAGIP	PIGNATI	Last name of the original Pigman
SECURS	CURSES	What do @#$% and 3@#$% represent in John's writing?
GOSLYCOYPH	PSYCHOLOGY	Lorraine reads a lot of books about ___.
SEKJO	JOKES	John no longer plays many practical ___.
DOOHHLCDI	CHILDHOOD	A Pigman basically kills a kid's ___.
LODLY	DOLLY	Ms. Racinski's first name
REBO	BORE	How does John refer to his father?
PACSHNI	SPINACH	Kind of cigarettes Lorraine wants John to smoke
STOPLIEREGT	POLTERGEIST	A mischievous ghost
TRAICEEFA	CAFETERIA	Dolly works in the school _____.
LEINODAML	MEDALLION	What was the Colonel wearing around his neck?
SUG	GUS	Phony name originally given by the Colonel
CAATTNIL	ATLANTIC	The Colonel wanted to go to ___ City.
RIS	IRS	What government agency does the Colonel fear most?
GOSETSRAUUS	STEGOSAURUS	Dinosaur with bony plates on its back
ALUP	PAUL	First name of author
GUFED	FUDGE	Gift that John and Lorraine took to the Colonel
WEDNES	SWEDEN	The Colonel was knighted by the King of ____.
FILE	LIFE	The only game the Colonel knows is The Game of ___.
KABUTSDEER	STUDEBAKER	Kind of car owned by the Colonel
ONTSHEENIR	RHINESTONE	Dolly wore what kind of earrings?
ROUF	FOUR	Dolly and the Colonel won ___ Thousand Dollars.
WOLEYL	YELLOW	Color of the Colonel's car
TPDEESRYINI	SERENDIPITY	Faculty of making fortunate discoveries by accident
LNNCOA	CONLAN	John's last name
STRIPE	PRIEST	Who did the Colonel ask to see before he died?
SOMEIRP	PROMISE	Name of the introduction to the book, The ___
ENLIVLLEG	GLENVILLE	Colonel's real last name
ARFB	BARF	Word John uses to be 'throw up'
MAGNER	GERMAN	Gus is a ___ shepherd.
MOTB	TOMB	A mausoleum is a large, stately ___.
HOGEK	KEOGH	A retirement plan for the self-employed
ECNEECOLDAS	ADOLESCENCE	Period from puberty to maturity

VOCABULARY RESOURCES

VOCABULARY WORD SEARCH - THE PIGMAN'S LEGACY

Words are placed backwards, forward, diagonally, up and down. Words listed below are included in the maze. Circle the hidden vocabulary words in the maze.

```
D E T R U L B S T U P O R N A I V E M Y
I C N R E P T G E S H R I N E T P R A H
L N E F X G L Y S R M M G H G I L A U V
A E G R V D R J W T E U E G C F N C S B
P C I D F I B E P I I N T M L F O I O W
I S D E P S P K T S D M D E O A I D L R
D E N T Z C K F H S D O U I D R S E E N
A L I R E I S S O D T R W L P G I M U Z
T O F E C P H N N S I L E G A I V A M V
E D O V S L G E H W S G E V R T T X L W
D A I N T E O M N Q W I N G E U I Y Y Z
S W B I A G E O L O G Y L I A R F N V M
B Z L H S Z K I M M E R S E T C I F G L
C P E K Y R E F I N E R I E S E Y E V C
C T S Y A B S T I N E N C E B D D Q Y W
D Y R R L C D V K Z C Q T C D Y P J D M
K G P V S X Q F X P V S F T R G C P S V
S R Z G K G Y H L S G J W M J S G F N W
M B V J N B M W B J K L F G P V P G T X
Z G S K B B C T F G Z H Q R W P K B D C
```

ABSTINENCE	EPIC	IMMERSE	MUTE	
ADOLESCENCE	FOIBLES	INDIGENT	NAIVE	STUPOR
ANGUISH	FOSSIL	INVERTED	OMEN	VISION
BLURTED	FRAIL	KEOGH	REFINERIES	WIDOW
DILAPIDATED	GEOLOGY	LEGACY	REGRETS	
DISCIPLE	GRAFFITI	MAUSOLEUM	REVERIE	
DOSSIER	GRUFF	MEDICARE	SERENDIPITY	
ECSTASY	IGNITED	MEMORIAL	SHRINE	
			STIMULATING	

WORD SEARCH ANSWER KEY - THE PIGMAN'S LEGACY

```
| D E T R U L B S T U P O R N A I V E M |
| I C N   E       E S H R I N E T P R A |
| L N E     G       S R M M G     I A U |
| A E G     D R   W T E U E   C F N C S |
| P C I D   I   E   I I N T M   F O I O |
| I S D E   S     T S D M D E O A I D L |
| D E N T   C   F H S   O U I   R S E E |
| A L I R E I S S O D   R W L P G I M U |
| T O F E C P H N   S I L E G A I V A M |
| E D O V S L G E     S G E V R T T   L |
| D A I N T E O M       I N G E U I Y   |
|     B I A G E O L O G Y L I A R F N   |
|     L   S   K I M M E R S E T C I F G |
|     E   Y R E F I N E R I E S E Y E   |
|     S   A B S T I N E N C E     D     |
```

Pigman's Legacy Vocabulary Crossword

Across
3. Skeleton or leaf imprint
5. Hypnotized
10. Retirement plan for the self-employed
11. Sigh of future good or evil
12. A large stately tomb
13. Delight
16. Said
21. Lit up
23. Experience of seeing the supernatural as if with the eyes
24. Not substantial; slight
25. Silent; unable to speak
26. Literary work that suggests epic grandeur or heroics
27. Come to become stonelike; to deaden
28. Feels sorry about
29. Site revered for its associations

Down
1. Cover completely in something else
2. Science of the origin, history and structure of the earth
4. Something handed down, as from an ancestor
6. Commemorating, serving as a reminder of
7. Impulsive
8. Collection of papers about a particular person
9. Reaching or having reached puberty
14. Daze
15. Agonizing physical or mental pain
17. Making a wavelike movement
18. Assistant; follower
19. A colorless artificial gem of paste or glass
20. Carved or etched into a surface
21. Turned inside out or up and down
22. People who look and behave like robots

Pigman's Legacy Vocabulary Crossword Answer Key

Across
- 3. Skeleton or leaf imprint
- 5. Hypnotized
- 10. Retirement plan for the self-employed
- 11. Sigh of future good or evil
- 12. A large stately tomb
- 13. Delight
- 16. Said
- 21. Lit up
- 23. Experience of seeing the supernatural as if with the eyes
- 24. Not substantial; slight
- 25. Silent; unable to speak
- 26. Literary work that suggests epic grandeur or heroics
- 27. Come to become stonelike; to deaden
- 28. Feels sorry about
- 29. Site revered for its associations

Down
- 1. Cover completely in something else
- 2. Science of the origin, history and structure of the earth
- 4. Something handed down, as from an ancestor
- 6. Commemorating, serving as a reminder of
- 7. Impulsive
- 8. Collection of papers about a particular person
- 9. Reaching or having reached puberty
- 14. Daze
- 15. Agonizing physical or mental pain
- 17. Making a wavelike movement
- 18. Assistant; follower
- 19. A colorless artificial gem of paste or glass
- 20. Carved or etched into a surface
- 21. Turned inside out or up and down
- 22. People who look and behave like robots

VOCABULARY WORKSHEET 1 - The Pigman's Legacy

___ 1. WHEEZE A. Overlook; forgive; disregard
___ 2. FLEECING B. Ability to make fortunate discoveries by accident
___ 3. TRESPASSING C. In disrepair, deterioration, or ruin
___ 4. WIDOW D. Minor weaknesses or failings of character
___ 5. FRAIL E. Government program for medical care for those over 65
___ 6. SERENDIPITY F. Come to become stonelike; to deaden
___ 7. LEGACY G. Defrauding of money or property; swindling
___ 8. CONVENT H. Not substantial; slight
___ 9. OMEN I. Hoarse whistling sound
___10. MANNEQUINS J. Science of the origin, history and structure of the earth
___11. BLURTED K. Woman whose husband has died
___12. CONDONE L. In a lively way
___13. DILAPIDATED M. Deliberate restraining of oneself; not indulging
___14. ENGRAVED N. Delight
___15. UNDULATING O. Invading the property rights of another
___16. KEOGH P. Said
___17. MEDICARE Q. Retirement plan for the self-employed
___18. VISION R. Dummies
___19. PERKILY S. A monastic community or house, especially of nuns
___20. ABSTINENCE T. Carved or etched into a surface
___21. ECSTASY U. Something handed down, as from an ancestor
___22. GEOLOGY V. Making a wavelike movement
___23. PETRIFY W. Sigh of future good or evil
___24. VIVACIOUSNESS X. Experience of seeing the supernatural as if with the eyes
___25. FOIBLES Y. Liveliness; spiritedness; animation

KEY: VOCABULARY WORKSHEET 1 - The Pigman's Legacy

I - 1.	WHEEZE	A. Overlook; forgive; disregard
G - 2.	FLEECING	B. Ability to make fortunate discoveries by accident
O - 3.	TRESPASSING	C. In disrepair, deterioration, or ruin
K - 4.	WIDOW	D. Minor weaknesses or failings of character
H - 5.	FRAIL	E. Government program for medical care for those over 65
B - 6.	SERENDIPITY	F. Come to become stonelike; to deaden
U - 7.	LEGACY	G. Defrauding of money or property; swindling
S - 8.	CONVENT	H. Not substantial; slight
W 9.	OMEN	I. Hoarse whistling sound
R -10.	MANNEQUINS	J. Science of the origin, history and structure of the earth
P -11.	BLURTED	K. Woman whose husband has died
A -12.	CONDONE	L. In a lively way
C -13.	DILAPIDATED	M. Deliberate restraining of oneself; not indulging
T -14.	ENGRAVED	N. Delight
V -15.	UNDULATING	O. Invading the property rights of another
Q -16.	KEOGH	P. Said
E -17.	MEDICARE	Q. Retirement plan for the self-employed
X -18.	VISION	R. Dummies
L -19.	PERKILY	S. A monastic community or house, especially of nuns
M -20.	ABSTINENCE	T. Carved or etched into a surface
N -21.	ECSTASY	U. Something handed down, as from an ancestor
J -22.	GEOLOGY	V. Making a wavelike movement
F -23.	PETRIFY	W. Sigh of future good or evil
Y -24.	VIVACIOUSNESS	X. Experience of seeing the supernatural as if with the eyes
D -25.	FOIBLES	Y. Liveliness; spiritedness; animation

VOCABULARY WORKSHEET 2 - The Pigman's Legacy

___ 1. FRAIL   A. A large stately tomb
___ 2. TRESPASSING   B. Turned inside out or up and down
___ 3. VISION   C. Settling without legal claim
___ 4. CONVENT   D. Reaching or having reached puberty
___ 5. SURREPTITIOUSLY   E. Feels sorry about
___ 6. MAUSOLEUM   F. Brief and unfriendly; harsh
___ 7. INVERTED   G. Minor weaknesses or failings of character
___ 8. CONVICTION   H. Dummies
___ 9. MANNEQUINS   I. Invading the property rights of another
___10. REINCARNATED   J. Silent; unable to speak
___11. SQUATTING   K. Skeleton or leaf imprint
___12. MESMERIZED   L. Formation of blood clot in a vessel or the heart
___13. VIVACIOUSNESS   M. Woman whose husband has died
___14. GRUFF   N. Strong belief
___15. FOSSIL   O. Site revered for its associations
___16. MUTE   P. Not substantial; slight
___17. SHRINE   Q. Reborn
___18. LIMITATIONS   R. Liveliness; spiritedness; animation
___19. LEGACY   S. Hypnotized
___20. WIDOW   T. Something handed down, as from an ancestor
___21. REGRETS   U. Restrictions; boundaries
___22. PUBESCENT   V. A monastic community or house, especially of nuns
___23. FOIBLES   W. Secretly
___24. THROMBOSIS   X. Agonizing physical or mental pain
___25. ANGUISH   Y. Experience of seeing the supernatural as if with the eyes

KEY: VOCABULARY WORKSHEET 2 - The Pigman's Legacy

P - 1.	FRAIL	A. A large stately tomb
I - 2.	TRESPASSING	B. Turned inside out or up and down
Y - 3.	VISION	C. Settling without legal claim
V - 4.	CONVENT	D. Reaching or having reached puberty
W - 5.	SURREPTITIOUSLY	E. Feels sorry about
A - 6.	MAUSOLEUM	F. Brief and unfriendly; harsh
B - 7.	INVERTED	G. Minor weaknesses or failings of character
N - 8.	CONVICTION	H. Dummies
H - 9.	MANNEQUINS	I. Invading the property rights of another
Q - 10.	REINCARNATED	J. Silent; unable to speak
C - 11.	SQUATTING	K. Skeleton or leaf imprint
S - 12.	MESMERIZED	L. Formation of blood clot in a vessel or the heart
R - 13.	VIVACIOUSNESS	M. Woman whose husband has died
F - 14.	GRUFF	N. Strong belief
K - 15.	FOSSIL	O. Site revered for its associations
J - 16.	MUTE	P. Not substantial; slight
O - 17.	SHRINE	Q. Reborn
U - 18.	LIMITATIONS	R. Liveliness; spiritedness; animation
T - 19.	LEGACY	S. Hypnotized
M - 20.	WIDOW	T. Something handed down, as from an ancestor
E - 21.	REGRETS	U. Restrictions; boundaries
D - 22.	PUBESCENT	V. A monastic community or house, especially of nuns
G - 23.	FOIBLES	W. Secretly
L - 24.	THROMBOSIS	X. Agonizing physical or mental pain
X - 25.	ANGUISH	Y. Experience of seeing the supernatural as if with the eyes

VOCABULARY JUGGLE LETTER REVIEW GAME - THE PIGMAN'S LEGACY

ROMMLAIE	MEMORIAL	Commemorating, serving as a reminder of
PECI	EPIC	Literary work that suggests epic grandeur or heroics
BESLOFI	FOIBLES	Minor weaknesses or failings of character
TRIAFFIG	GRAFFITI	Drawing or inscription on wall or other surface
DOONECN	CONDONE	Overlook; forgive; disregard
CYOSHYOPLG	PSYCHOLOGY	Science that deals with mental processes and behavior
SEMERIM	IMMERSE	Cover completely in something else
LNUGITANUD	UNDULATING	Making a wavelike movement
TENBECPUS	PUBESCENT	Reaching or having reached puberty
CEGAYL	LEGACY	Something handed down, as from an ancestor
NALYLAPOLCIT	PLATONICALLY	Transcending physical desire; spiritual
GLEFCIEN	FLEECING	Defrauding of money or property; swindling
REUSGBEMD	SUBMERGED	Under; beneath
VONETNC	CONVENT	A monastic community or house, especially of nuns
SHIRENOTEN	RHINESTONE	A colorless artificial gem of paste or glass
RIOPTANAIP	APPARITION	A ghost
WOWID	WIDOW	Woman whose husband has died
BRISTMHOOS	THROMBOSIS	Formation of blood clot in a vessel or the heart
STANGRISESP	TRESPASSING	Invading the property rights of another
GLIMTUSNATI	STIMULATING	Exciting
SEEDCENOLAC	ADOLESCENCE	Period from puberty to maturity; teen years
RITYPEF	PETRIFY	Come to become stonelike; to deaden
RISHEN	SHRINE	Site revered for its associations
LARFI	FRAIL	Not substantial; slight
FGFRU	GRUFF	brief and unfriendly; harsh
AQITNTGSU	SQUATTING	Settling without legal claim
EHEZEW	WHEEZE	Hoarse whistling sound
SRIEDOS	DOSSIER	Collection of papers about a particular person
PEDALIDTAID	DILAPIDATED	In disrepair, deterioration, or ruin
NERIREDTACAN	REINCARNATED	Reborn
PORUTS	STUPOR	Site revered for its associations
QNENASMIUN	MANNEQUINS	Dummies
LOMENILAD	MEDALLION	A large medal
SLOIFS	FOSSIL	Skeleton or leaf imprint
VRAENDEG	ENGRAVED	Carved or etched into a surface
LOOYEGG	GEOLOGY	Science of the origin, history and structure of the earth
VAINE	NAIVE	Simple; lacking in worldliness and sophistication
SOVINI	VISION	Experience of seeing the supernatural as if with the eyes
MNOE	OMEN	Sign of future good or evil

REERVEI	REVERIE	A state of abstract musing
GINITNED	INDIGENT	Impoverished; needy
GOSSRUTEAUS	STEGOSAURUS	Dinosaur with a double row of bony plates on its back
MOLAUUMES	MAUSOLEUM	A large stately tomb
TRIMODIEF	MORTIFIED	Humiliated; shamed
GHANISU	ANGUISH	Agonizing physical or mental pain
CRAEIDEM	MEDICARE	Government program for medical care for those over 65
GEOHK	KEOGH	Retirement plan for the self-employed
KELYRIP	PERKILY	In a lively way
NITONCOCIV	CONVICTION	Strong belief
NCENBATIES	ABSTINENCE	Deliberate restraining of oneself; not indulging
SAVVISEOUCINS	VIVACIOUSNESS	Liveliness; spiritedness; animation
BIOZEMS	ZOMBIES	People who look and behave like robots
SCYSATE	ECSTASY	Delight
PIDEISLC	DISCIPLE	Assistant; follower
REDUTLB	BLURTED	Said
TVNIDEER	INVERTED	Turned inside out or up and down
GESTRER	REGRETS	Feels sorry about
INERERFSIE	REFINERIES	Plants that purify crude substances
TUME	MUTE	Silent; unable to speak
ITLINSATOMI	LIMITATIONS	Restrictions; boundaries
TRESSENYPIDI	SERENDIPITY	Ability to make fortunate discoveries by accident
NEDITIG	IGNITED	Lit up
ISVIENNTTIC	INSTINCTIVE	Impulsive
ZMEMEEDRIS	MESMERIZED	Hypnotized

www.ingramcontent.com/pod-product-compliance
Lightning Source LLC
Chambersburg PA
CBHW051411070526
44584CB00023B/3381